Take Back Your News
Clearing away the rubble

by

Stephen B. Waters

Published by:
Stephen Waters
Rome, NY

© 2018 Stephen B. Waters, Rome, NY USA
First Edition, printed in paperback

All rights reserved. No part of this book may be reproduced in any form or by any electronic or mechanical means, including recording and information storage and retrieval systems without permission in writing from the publisher, except by a reviewer, who may quote brief passages in a review.

Any members of educational institutions wishing to photocopy part or all of the work for classroom use, or publishers who would like to obtain permission to include the work in an anthology, should send their inquiries the publisher at the address below.

Printed in the United States of America

Waters, Stephen B.
    Take Back Your News/ Stephen B. Waters
    ISBN-13: 978-0-9845258-3-6 (Paperback)
    ISBN-13: 978-0-9845258-4-3 (Hardcover)
        Library of Congress Control Number: 2018901883

    File under non-fiction.

Published by:
    Stephen Waters
    6391 Karlen Rd.
    Rome, NY 13440
VC

Table of Contents

DEDICATION V
INTRODUCTION VII

BOOK 1: CLEARING AWAY THE RUBBLE 1
   How to defend against poor journalism *10*
   Inoculating against media failure *10*
   Why care about journalism? *11*
   How journalism dug us into a hole *13*
   News is specific *15*

EVIDENCE: WORDS MATTER 19
   Media misuse words to substitute how they feel *19*
   Media adjectives and adverbs editorialize *22*
   Media labels push a political agenda *23*
   Media descriptives and logical fallacies color reporting *24*
   Media manufacture messages *25*
   Media plant Improvised Editorial Devices (IEDs) *27*
   Media confuse readers with jargon *27*
   Media postmodernize word meanings *31*
EVIDENCE: MEDIA SELL OPINION AS NEWS 33
   Media equivocate to register opinion *36*
   Media push emotional opinion *37*
   Media speculate, project and guess *38*
   Media push unsubstantiated accusations *39*
   Media let personal views interfere *42*
EVIDENCE: MEDIA ACCENTUATE NARRATIVES 43
   Media focus their lens to affect stories *43*
   Media maps lose accuracy when details are massaged *45*
   Media manipulate context *46*
   Media compress past and present to warp context *49*
   Media preconceived narratives replace news *51*

    Media push Agitprop as news *53*
    Media fact-starved "fact-checking" isn't news *54*
  EVIDENCE: MEDIA OBSCURE NEWS *54*
    Media substitute Information for news *54*
    Media use headlines to obscure *55*
    Media misidentify content to avoid reporting *57*
    Media engage in willful ignorance *58*
    Media omit real news *59*
    Media misdirect readers *61*
    Media misdirect with innuendo *62*
    Media warp with selectively reporting *63*
    Media selectively misquote *64*
    Media breaking news is often theater *67*
    Media proffer noise as news *67*
    Media replace news with noise *71*
BOOK 2: HOW SCHOOLS FAIL JOURNALISM *77*
    1. Social Studies: To whom does an education belong? *77*
    2. Social Studies: To educate or to school? *79*
    3. Social Studies: A culture war *81*
    4. Social Studies: Key understandings go beyond culture *82*
    5. Social Studies: unencumbered with principles *84*
    6. Social Studies: Irrelevant themes *86*
    7. Social Studies: Specifications that misdirect *88*
    8. Social Studies: Practices that obscure history *90*
    9. Social Studies: The battle for individuals in society *93*
    10. Social Studies: Social transformation is not education .. *95*
    Social Studies: In summary, bring on laughter *97*

BOOK 3: WHERE NEWS FITS IN SOCIETY *99*
    The Fabric of Society *99*
    1. Educating Individuals *100*
    2. Individuals create society *102*
    3. Individuals relate to culture through society *106*
    4. Individuals mature using dynamic processes *108*
    5. Individuals were haphazardly taught character *110*
    6. Individuals use experience to produce character *112*
    7. How individual character blossoms *114*
    8. Individuals validate character *116*
    9. Individual principles matter *118*

10. Individuals validate governance 121
11. Taking individual responsibility 123
12. Individuals find meaning 125
13. Individuals find their place in society 127
14. Individuals prepare for the future 129

A JOURNALISM TO EMBRACE 133

APPENDIX 1 — TRUMP ROME, NY CAMPAIGN COVERAGE 137
APPENDIX 2 — STATE OF THE UNION ADDRESS 141
APPENDIX 3 — QUESTIONS THAT NURTURE THINKING 145

Dedication

Great, great grandfather, Augustus C. Kessinger, started work at the Rome (NY) Sentinel in 1854 as a printer's devil, breaking down pages to reclaim and re-case individual letters of type for use the next week. Type was expensive. You might say that words were valuable back then. Not so much anymore.

Our family still believes words matter. Since A.C., six generations of our family have held the newspaper in stewardship for our community.

This is dedicated to more than 150 years of staff who worked diligently to reflect community back to individuals who create it.

Together we have helped grow livelihood, quality of life, and a safe place for family and friends. Who could ask for more?

Introduction

While a newspaper article about Donald Trump appears on the cover, this book is about the media, not Trump. We have replaced Trump's picture that ran in the newspaper with a picture of the media that poorly reported Trump's rally.

#FakeNews is a misplaced notion. #FakeJournalism is a more persistent problem.

Trump dared point out that poor national reporting worsens the political, economic, and social problems faced by our country. The media wrongly criticized him for that.

This book would be unnecessary if:

- More journalists understood their craft,
- More readers/viewers took responsibility for their news,
- More people understood how to choose experts.
- More teachers understood their obligation to students,
- More public officials understood society,

Start the book anywhere. Journalism, schooling, and society all need your help. In Book 1, mine the evidence of poor journalistic practice gathered during the 2016 presidential campaign and judge its quality for yourself.

In Book 2 see how schools shortchange students so they seldom notice poor journalistic practice or government.

In Book 3 look at society and its principles, the better to sort through noise flung at us.

Some points repeat in the books because they were first written as standalone articles based on my 2010 book, *Individuals, Journalism, and Society*.

Book 1: Clearing away the rubble

News can fail you so many ways.

Actually, those who gather news can fail you by how they write and what they say.

The structure and integrity of news can fail through words, phrases, order, focus, scope, selection, omission, misrepresentation, juxtaposition, inference, innuendo, and much more.

Those who benefit from preserving their media fiefdom in proximity to power won't confess their frailty. Their instinct for self-preservation results in many not taking responsibility for content. Past performance gives little reason to trust their instincts.

Journalism is an accolade that must be earned fresh each day. Within a single article a clinker sentence may follow an excellent paragraph. An excellent article may be located next to junk. Too few readers and viewers seem to hold the press accountable for what they deliver.

A recent article said that X preferred immigrants from one country to those of another. Our wire service added a clause to the article that promoted a popular media narrative.

Where did the clause come from? Did X say what the wire service implied? Did an unnamed source add spin? Did the reporter embellish the remark? Why did the wire service leave out official statements that made the clause irrelevant?

The article was a hit job in three ways. First, editors appeared not to care enough about accuracy in news to clarify their inference.

Second, and the article's real outrage, was to misdirect the reader from news whether a pending political compromise could be reached in a timely fashion. The writer rhetorically focused on an incidental remark to create conflict and drama.

Take Back Your News

Third, combined national media chose to megaphone outrage that resulted from their coverage. Just as Hollywood air kisses obscure rot and Washington overlooks its own abuse, the informal media craft guild protects its own. Institutional blindness seems to sap willingness to right the ship.

How did we get into the mess in the first place? Who trained these journalists? How were they schooled? How were readers schooled to overlook problems in one of our culture's essential institutions? What can be done about it?

Many claim a journalist's duty is to "afflict the comfortable and comfort the afflicted."

Not so. The press should report news. Media that afflicts the comfortable and comforts the afflicted *instead* of reporting news is dispensable. Finley Peter Dunne who coined the phrase meant it as a criticism, not a goal.

In 1902, Dunne, a Chicago reporter and editor, took misguided muckraking journalism to task for misplaced zealotry.[1] His popular character "Dooley" punctured the self-important hypocrisy of muckraking:

> *"Th newspaper does ivrything f'r us. It runs th' polis foorce an' th' banks, commands th' milishy, controls th' ligislachure, baptizes th' young, marries th' foolish,* **comforts th' afflicted, afflicts th' comfortable***, buries th' dead an' roasts thim aftherward".*[2]

Dunne derided reporters who wanted their judgments to matter more than the judgment of readers.

Dooley today might warn to readers: *"Jest because ya hears sumpth'n don't make it worth list'nin' to."*

Press representations of what matters are too often casually accepted. Whatever one thinks of Donald Trump, he forced both the press and consumers to face those miss-representations:

> RealDonaldTrump 5:02 AM - 13 Dec 2017: Wow, more than 90% of Fake News Media coverage of me is negative, with numerous forced retractions

---

[1] In the 1960 film, Inherit the Wind. Gene Kelly as E.K. Hornbeck says, "Mr. Brady, it is the duty of a newspaper to comfort the afflicted and afflict the comfortable".
[2] Dunne, Finley Peter. *Observations by Mr. Dooley* (1902)

Clearing away the rubble

of untrue stories. Hence my use of Social Media, the only way to get the truth out.

Ironically, our newspaper emailed our wire service that day:

How quickly real news descends into narrative:
[Wire Service]: Two FBI officials who would later be assigned to the special counsel's **investigation into Donald Trump's presidential campaign** . . .
What we ran: Two FBI officials who would later be assigned to the special counsel's **investigation into possible Russian collusion in the 2016 election** . . .
Please try to present the news most accurately.

The wire service had seeded articles with representations that nudged readers toward erroneous assumptions.

Somehow many in the press decided not to report news, but to substitute judgment. Quite simply, CNN, MSNBC, NBC, CBS, ABC, NPR, and national newspapers like the New York *Times* and *Washington Post* practice advocacy. Similar patterns of abuse can be found across the political spectrum. Fox Business can sometimes seem as strident and opinionated as CNN.

For all the noise at the national level, a greater problem flies under the radar. Thousands of newspapers every day are fed wire service articles that contain demonstrably poor journalism.

Wire services have an opportunity to engage in verbal theater, blindly accept opposition talking points, and repeat memes they call context. They can proffer unchallenged narratives, self-supporting facts, and embellish prose with decorations.

President Ronald Reagan's "Trust but verify" warning should apply to the press, whether progressive, liberal, moderate, or conservative and reported in print, television, or online.

It's long overdue. Trust but verify would have helped in 1968 when Walter Cronkite during the Viet Cong Tet Offensive passed his opinion off as news, claiming the American situation was unwinnable. Trust but verify would have helped during the 2004 presidential campaign when Dan Rather presented likely forged documentation on George W. Bush's Texas National Guard experience.

Trust but verify would help now.

Our newspaper publishes national and international news like other newspapers do, but re-edit it before we run it.

Before drinking, hikers filter water from woodland streams to remove hazards. Local newspapers — and readers — should filter wire service copy to remove detritus before serving it.

We have repeatedly advised wire service managers they should better filter content before they ship it out.

It's up to us, then, and ultimately, up to readers to find patterns in reporting. Then decide whether you are presented with news or with a media version of what they want you to believe.

The 2016 presidential campaign unfolded with more than a dozen candidates vying for nominations and election. Our staff and management had no favorite, and no interest in having one. We were interested in solid reporting that would give our readers sound basis for making their own judgments come Election Day.

The days of Republican and Democrat partisan reporting disappeared in the late 1940s — or so we thought — when everyone laughed at the Chicago *Tribune* headline that Dewey beat Truman when the opposite was true.

Our newspaper was registered as an Independent Democrat back when FDR, was governor of New York and he wrote letters to us signed, "Frank." Great-grandfather ran for Congress in 1924 as a Democrat. Nelson Rockefeller, a liberal Republican, was on a first name basis with our parents. Owners of our family-owned newspaper have been both long-time Democrats and long-time Republicans.

Editorially, we tended to speak on issues rather than support particular candidates from either party. The newsroom reports news independent of editorial position and squarely down the middle. For the longest time we passed along wire service reporting to readers virtually unchanged.

Then presidential candidate Donald Trump came to town April 12, 2016.

Trump seems to cause people to unmask themselves. He pushed the mainstream media (MSM) to reveal they are in business to stay

Clearing away the rubble

in business and not necessarily in business to serve readers news. If they can keep you coming back, they don't need to report news to succeed.

The evidence at the end of this chapter shows how and where the mainstream media colors reporting. Too much media "Whataboutism" is as useless as beating a "you're being lied to" drum. Neither compels a move closer to understanding. Neither serves readers and viewers.

Discussion requires one to accurately, concisely, and completely present a position and respond to it. Replying instead with rhetorical hand grenades substitutes obfuscation for discussion. When "winning" becomes so important that context, facts, and understanding get corrupted, you can't win. In fact, you already have lost.

Powerful people co-opt those whom they would influence. They interbreed with the media, feed it scraps, favor preferred reporters and pundits, and, in return, expect to be treated deferentially.

Centuries ago Europeans considered three estates to be the centers of power: clergy, nobility, and commoners. The United States Constitution replaced those centers of power with three branches of government: the legislature, the executive, and the judiciary. The press later began being called the "Fourth Estate" — an inflated term for those who exercise political influence through journalism.

Regulatory capture happens when businesses overseen by government agencies populate an agency with staff beholden to them. Government does not manage national media through regulatory capture, but dividends are paid for media personalities to curry favor with officials.

Politicians exert power over the national press and over other institutions. Education feels the gravity of those who exercise the levers of education. They demand requirements, direct schooling, and squeeze content in or out. It's all the same. Schools are an incubator for later media problems.

The Soviet government controlled schooling and the press. Alexander Solzhenitsyn described the unofficial *Samizdat* press that rose to counter official soviet media. Faced not with a controlled press, but a compliant press, many Americans have turned to social media—blogs, twitter, Facebook, and the like — to fulfill the *samizdat* function of more thoroughly vetting news.

Individuals schooled more than educated will not see the need to weigh in if they don't recognize the press is broken. Those in power consider Trump's use of social media to be "unpresidential" when it dares to point out how the press fails.

The mainstream media, including our wire service, chastise Trump for tweets because tweets bypass media power and influence. Trump tweets to make individuals aware of what is written and challenges people to face those shortcomings.

Ours is a small, family-owned newspaper in upstate New York. Independent daily newspapers like ours are a rarity in corporate-dominated media. A throwback to the last century, independents tend to pay attention to news while corporate-owned newspapers are more focused on the bottom line.

Misreporting news became forcefully evident to us at Trump's Rome campaign rally. Major news media like CNN, the alphabet TV networks, major newspapers, and wire services filled tiers of risers in back of the crowd of 5,000.

Our wire service distilled the campaign rally to a single sentence:
> "At a rally in Rome, New York, Tuesday evening, Trump angrily denounced Saturday's final allocation of all of Colorado's delegates to Cruz, blasting the party's system as 'rigged' and 'corrupt.'"

The single sentence was buried deep in the 32-paragraph, 893-word wire service report. The sentence was buried so deep most newspaper editors probably cut it for length unaware the media had cheated readers of Trump's substance. They cheated readers of news. In its place they delivered information and opinion.

News is specific. News is not just information. News is a well-defined subset of information. News is what you need to know to plan your future better.

News is not, for instance, that Republican presidential candidate Donald J. Trump campaigned before a crowd in Rome, NY. News is what Trump *said* to the crowd. It is news because those elsewhere needed to learn enough to decide for whom to vote.

The distinction between news, information, and opinion matters:
- **News**: is what you need to know — "There might be a hole where you are about to walk."
- **Information**: while it may be true, is not news — "Lots of people like ice cream."
- **Opinion**: whether true or false, is not news — "I like ice cream."

The old joke about small-town newspapers is that readers buy the Saturday edition to see if, after the Friday night football game, the paper accurately reported what happened.

Readers hire local newspapers to do what they are too busy to do:
- Record who was born, married, and died
- Report local government, meetings, public safety news
- Select useful articles from national wire services

We reported details to our readers. We reported what was said at the rally that readers needed to know:

> Trump hit hard in repetitive Twitter length phrases:
> "Nobody is voting for a third term for Obama!"
> "In Benghazi, Hillary never showed up for the 3 AM call."
> "The three most important problems are security, security, and security!"
> "Many countries are not carrying their weight!"
> "You always have to be prepared to walk away when you deal."
> "I'll be slow on the trigger, but no one will mess with us."
> "No one respects women more than Donald Trump!" although "these liars in the media behind you" won't say that.
> Repeatedly he hit the national media. "I have the smartest people and the most loyal. Even the liars back there will say that."
> And about Washington politicians, including the GOP establishment trying to derail his campaign, "Every single one of these people are controlling!"
> Trump accused the GOP elite and pundits of saying he could not win the election, "but they said I couldn't win primaries either."

By inserting themselves between newsworthy events and readers, the national media saw themselves as arbiters of what happened.

Trump exposed the scam. He nudged the audience to recognize that the business of mainstream media isn't news, but rather styling information and opinion as if the media mattered more than news.

The media were outraged Trump dared point it out. The media wrapped itself in the First Amendment to preserve their franchise. They claimed those who challenged their journalistic integrity were opposed to a free press. That's dramatic, but wrong.

A century ago, canaries were carried into coalmines to warn miners of failing air quality. Journalism's canary had died and Trump dared point it out. The media portrayed a façade of being the essential reliable source of news when it had made itself irrelevant.

Compare journalism to large people-moving networks fixed in place long ago when cities were in their infancy. New transportation systems designed today would work more efficiently and effectively than those fixed in place long ago. Media word-moving networks, also set up back when cities were maturing, inconvenience people as much as dated physical transportation networks do. They don't meet our needs efficiently but are what we are obliged to work with.

When you can identify patterns in journalism, you can label them, laugh at them, and defend against them. A special place in Danté's *Inferno* should be reserved for abusers of journalism. Blunders that infect journalism were described in *Individuals, Journalism and Society*[3].

Here is a sample:

Abused language — Adjectives and nouns matter. Resorting to euphemisms, mislabeling or selective labeling has consequences.

Astroturf —Applying the media lens to staged demonstrations even when chanted clichés are juvenile, pathetic, and nonsensical.

Blinders — Reporting an artificially limited scope cheats readers of insight others offer.

Celebrity fetishism — People known for knowness displayed as if they have special expertise.

Contrived accents — Article placement, fact placement, all affect emphasis.

Cronyism — Presenting views of other journalists as if news.

---

[3] Waters, Stephen B. *Individuals, Journalism, and Society*. 2010.

Clearing away the rubble

Echoing vicious noise — Serving noise intentionally inserted to derail discussion. Prune away the noise, don't amplify it.

False drama — Backdrops that suggest first hand knowledge without real evidence.

Gotcha journalism — Structuring a non-debatable view beforehand as the main storyline.

Gullibility — Promoting Photoshopped or staged pictures unchallenged.

Historical amnesia — Parroting popular fictions instead of solid research. For too many journalists today, history begins at dawn.

Junk science — Reporting scientific consensus is not bad science; it is no science.

Lack of focus — Reporting should not be an excuse to miss presenting issues clearly and accurately.

"Look! Squirrel!" — Real scandals get forgotten when overcome by shiny distractions.

Manufactured news — Non-events breathlessly fluffed into features.

Milestone reporting — Reporting events absent context as if themselves significant.

Misplaced judgment —Opinion held by journalists is not so special it should take the place of that of readers.

Misplaced tolerance — Journalists abdicate responsibility to label bad behavior for what it is. Mired in their own moral relativism, they seldom recognize abuse of individuals is always wrong.

Misrepresentation — Inaccurate and non-representative content covered because it exists.

Monday morning quarterbacking — Telling people what one should have said does not report what they said.

One-sided claims — Saying what one official says without evidence for context.

Outrageous Style — Emotional righteous indignation passed off as news.

Platitudes — Clichés sound good, but they are not principles, distilled from experience, tested over time, and projected into the future to test for plausibility. "Give peace a chance" is a platitude used to stop thinking, not a civil process to solve problems peaceably.

Pushing the narrative — Filtering what is reported to fit a preconceived notion.

Silence —Media seldom hold people accountable for what they previously said, or seldom cover why views have changed.

Mislabeling — The press regularly commits politics . . . which is okay, when readers and viewers understand it to be entertainment or opinion. The sin is suggesting it is news.

The clear purpose of this book is to galvanize people to reclaim news, for their own safety's sake.

Take Back Your News

Journalism is a craft and nothing special. Too much of what passes for reporting is a Twinkie™ — a soft, cakelike confection filled with an appealing creamy center. The book will succeed if we can turn some Twinkies into food that tastes good yet is better for you.

How to defend against poor journalism

One journalistic blunder is no more blunderous than another. Each perpetrates assault on readers. Media commits large and small assaults against journalism every day.

Hone identifying skills to defend against such blunders. See too many? Turn the page. Buy a different newspaper. Change the channel.

Local newspapers serve readers poorly when they print without editing and without validating wire service and national news media work product. *Iowahawk* David Burge chastised journalism:

> @iowahawkblog 6:57 AM - 9 May 2013
> Journalism is about covering important stories. With a pillow, until they stop moving.

Faced with consistent weak reporting, our newspaper resolved to do better. We identified slipshod work and emailed specific concerns and our corrections to the wire service.

Journalism broke, in part, because we assumed those who were credentialed to teach well were also expert about the content they were obliged to teach. Excellent teachers can pass on bilge as easily as excellent writers can do the same.

People can inoculate against media failure if they recalibrate what matters in individual lives, in journalism, and in society.

Inoculating against media failure

Our wire service ceased to report news when it began to insulate readers from what the candidate said.

The media reported *about* Trump's campaign speech rather than the speech itself. *Appendix 1* contains the full article filed by the wire service about Trump's Rome visit.

Clearing away the rubble

Not only did the wire service not report detail, they provided no summary, and no link to a transcript.

The offense has been repeated often. The wire service squeezed out almost all substance from President Trump's speech at the 72nd United Nations General Assembly. They labeled "news" what they failed to deliver.

A magician practices misdirection. One hand typically distracts while the other performs sleight of hand. When media focuses on information, omitted news is seldom missed.

For instance, who is ahead at the turn does not matter during a horse race or an election. Media magicians that draw attention to who is "ahead" during a campaign distract from what people need to know to decide for whom to vote.

News is a subset of information that offers what you need to know to plan your future better. Information and news overlap, but they are not identical.

Trump differentiates noise from news while media won't admit a difference. It has to sting for the media to be called out publicly for failing to do journalism.

Why care about journalism?

Individuals created journalism to help them collect, sift, and digest the complexity of the rest of the world.

Not all complexity matters. Some complexity is smoke in which public administration hides abuse, encourages abuse, adds intricacy, and obscures abusers. That is a centuries-old political/cultural problem a complacent media often chooses to ignore.

Journalism worked better when our grandparents were children because most newspapers were locally owned and edited by an independent and curmudgeonly lot. They held multiple wire services accountable for content.

Managers of the Associated Press—a member-owned cooperative wire service—told publishers back then, "You own us."

"Damn right we do," owner/editors replied. Quality reporting was expected. At annual national and state bureau meetings they held AP accountable for it.

Since 1950, the total number of daily newspapers dwindled from 1,772 to perhaps less than 1,300 today and corporate newspaper chains with different priorities swallowed many of those that remain. Their accountants eying the bottom line reduced the number and experience of reporters and editors. Numbers have diminished, and the quality, too.

Radio stations of the 1950s were often derided for a "rip-and-read" approach to wire service news. Staff tore wire service copy off the Teletype and, without looking at it first, read it unchanged and unedited on the air. Many newsrooms place copy on pages unchanged and unedited before printing. Local wire editors don't see a need to edit wire copy. Copy that is not reviewed at the local level gives national media a license to fail.

Credentialing of journalists has created a different problem. The credentialed consider themselves professional because other credentialed vouched for them. Credentials mean nothing more than that someone has run an academic gauntlet, regurgitating for professors what those scholars wanted to hear.

Credentials are no guarantee one can think any more than a degree in public administration guarantees one can govern or a degree in education guarantees one can teach.

Credentials are little more than the modern equivalent of medieval craft guilds that restricted entry into crafts, allowing only select and approved members to practice. They constructed a protected and privileged circumstance for their own benefit, while professing to hold themselves to high standards for the benefit of consumers.

Practitioners of the craft often wrap themselves in claims of privilege bestowing title to make judgments about what the rest of us should believe. In practice, a journalist is only as good as the article delivered today.

Clearing away the rubble

A concentration of media power has accentuated inbreeding and conformist views. National media seem not know how to get better or why they should.

Meanwhile, those who consume journalism face a different problem. Consumers are not lazy, but they are busy. Recent generations were schooled to put trust in experts. They defer to experts in government, politics, education, science and elsewhere. "Expert" has become perverted to mean someone with credentials and/or experience.

Actually, expertise is something more specific and practical:

> An expert is someone who explains things so clearly that even we can understand.

The only way to see the difference between real experts and those who unjustifiably claim expertise is to hold them accountable to explain themselves.

Most people don't do that. They hire a second set of experts called journalists to check their first set of experts. Too often, specialists selected to guard the guardians seemed not to understand what they were hired to do.

Having passed responsibility on to others, consumers get on with its busy lives, comfortable in the notion that all is well, even though it wasn't, isn't, and won't be.

How journalism dug us into a hole

The world has always been more complicated than any individual can know or understand. Still, some wizards claim almost magical insights absent proof.

They would use their rhetoric to instill specific beliefs in us. They urge us to be "good" citizens, defining "good" to their own satisfaction. Such pseudo-journalists believe their task is to make decisions for us, replacing news with personal or corporate views. That's not how it is supposed to work.

Truly humble reporters prefer to listen to many people thinking individually. Good journalists bring their skills to an assignment, but leave personal baggage at home. Good journalists approach an assignment without a preset narrative, applying their skills to the task but not their views. Journalists lose their purpose when they presume to shape civilization in their own image and warp their work.

To reclaim the news, readers and viewers need to step up as a necessary check and balance on journalism. One can't just trust a particular newspaper, channel, or website because of it's logo or slogan, because it is popular, because it coincides with personal beliefs, or because the current newsreader once was a decent journalist.

You know enough to vet journalists because you:
- Exercise judgment
- Ask questions
- Compare evidence
- Value words you hear and read
- Examine premises
- Consider whether conclusions logically follow from premises

You judge for every new article whether journalism is working. Repeating for emphasis: journalism is an accolade to be earned fresh with each article. Excellent journalism can sit next to junk.

The need to become expert enough to judge "journalism" or "junk" is not new. Dorothy Sayers, mystery writer, medievalist, and one of the first female Oxford University graduates, warned of the problem in 1948:

> "For we let our young men and women go out unarmed, in a day when armor was never so necessary. By teaching them all to read, we have left them at the mercy of the printed word. By the invention of the film and the radio, we have made certain that no aversion to reading shall secure them from the incessant battery of words, words, words. They do not know what the words mean; they do not know how to ward them off or blunt their edge or fling them back; they are a prey to words in their emotions instead of being the masters of them in their intellects."

Rather than heed her warning to academics, educationists doubled down, added trivial schooling requirements, and imposed unwise bureaucratic mandates that produced all-encompassing fog.

Fog is difficult to recognize when one is in the thick of it. It's like peripheral vision that ends somewhere unknown to us. Like

Clearing away the rubble

fog, people seldom notice where journalism ends without examining evidence. Once pointed out, patterns of poor journalism become easier to identify and label. The examples that follow show people need only master what once were everyday language skills to weed the garden of news on a daily basis.

Sensitized to patterns, it's possible to consider why they are no longer taught. A *post mortem* on recent common practice shows where schooling fails helps to inoculate us to defend ourselves.

Every day is an opportunity to measure individuals, journalism, and society.

News is specific

News is specific. News is what you need to know to plan your future better.

News is like a nautical chart—abbreviated but accurate in its essentials, omitting both artificial errors and extraneous noise. A ship's captain cannot trust a nautical chart that omits real shoals or one that inserts fake hazards. News, like a nautical chart, should not include every detail, but should, in the space available, represent details that are accurate and sufficient to be useful.

News is not casual. Its verbiage should be spare and accurate. Cavalier attachment of questionable adjectives should be avoided. For instance, the Congressional Budget Office (CBO) is often labeled "non-partisan" with the implication that the description somehow is authoritative and useful. The actual CBO track record is seldom reported.

- The CBO's Obamacare enrollment estimates made three years ago were wrong by 90 percent.
- The CBO gamed (colluded?) with Obama officials to game the original Obamacare numbers to fit the 10-year estimate.

Such purposely thin reporting delivers a tainted product to the detriment of citizens and the country.

Nor is it appropriate to blame technology for faulty news reporting. Semaphore, telegraph, radio, television, and the Internet all can transmit news. Bandwidth may have increased, but news is news independent of the medium. Technology hasn't "speeded things up" so people are overwhelmed. Noise does not overwhelm the signal. Individuals still choose how much of a glass of water to drink. They know enough not to swallow an entire lake at once.

Bandwidth and rate of transmission are significant in the everyday feedback loop of thought, but it is the feedback loop that matters. Feedback loops cycle signal, action, and relaxation damping before readying another cycle. Feedback loops are relegated to science classes, rather than Liberal Arts or the art of living.

Relaxation cycles of a feedback loop used to be fulfilled by technological limits. Now they are up to you. Brains are feedback systems. In feedback loops, *damping* is controlled either by technology or software. Brain software can adjust its approach to deal with high bandwidth.

In feedback loops, it is content that matters. Content itself is regularly abused. When pseudo-journalists tell us what to believe, or selectively inform us to drive belief toward their preferred beliefs, they practice postmodern word games to shape-shift politics. They try to be emotionally compelling but fail. Their game is fraud. Their robes and titles do not define them any more than their labels and associations define the rest of us.

They misunderstand how simple humanity and society really are. Even together we are still individual and alone—obliged to make of the universe what each of us can, while constrained as individuals to use tools that evolution has given us:

- Sense experience
- Pattern recognition
- Comparison and deduction

When postmodern elitists presume to know what is good for us, they forsake community. Selfishly, they destroy instead of build. To defend against the threat, good people need to recalibrate journalism to fill the job it was designed to do.

1) Journalism fits between individuals and society, and
2) Journalism reinforces basics of society that often get misunderstood

The 20th century was overtaken in part because institutions schooled people to believe centralized control and communication would be able to manage and preserve civil society with greater

Clearing away the rubble

success than previous centuries were able to accomplish using their systems of government. That view has not delivered stable civil institutions that benefit individuals who join together in society with others.

> The 16th century tried religion.
> The 17th century tried autocracy.
> The 18th century tried enlightenment.
> The 19th century tried industrialization.
> The 20th century tried centralized control with mass communication.

Individuals hire journalists, not governments, rulers, or firms.

To perpetuate itself, governments claimed responsibility for schools to devalue both individuals and journalism. Academic standards, implementations, or assessments are not the problem, but rather requirements that obscure and elbow aside what matters.

Before we get to Books 2 and 3 that speak to school shortcomings and society's needs, consider concrete examples that show the mainstream media is not as good as it should be. The examples point out news writing that has been sent regularly by wire services to most newspapers across the country. Where is the outrage?

Evidence of media failure

Evidence: Words matter

Media misuse words to substitute how they feel

Journalists sling words at readers that are crafted for impact. Programs are described as "reduced" for budget cuts writers favor, while other cuts they don't like are "slashed".

For the entire presidential campaign, Trump was "billionaire" who often visited his "palatial" resort at Mar-a-Lago, Florida. After he was elected, he still was referred to as "billionaire businessman" Donald Trump. We complained to the wire service:

> 1) Please drop "billionaire" from the [wire service] Trump lexicon. For variety, try "President elect" instead.

They still do it — using different words to repeat the same cheap rhetorical ploys.

Not just individual words, but phrases reappear week after week, month after month, and year after year. It goes unnoticed that they are shaping the battlefield of your mind.

Media choose words to color what happened. Rather than add context, repeated hammering advertises for the opposition. Reporters editorialize every time they insert unnecessary adjectives and adverbs to "punch up" a story.

Our email to the wire service July, 22, 2016, said:

> Hi, [Wire service rep]...
> [Wire service reporter] would benefit from editing that would tighten her reporting. It would tone down her penchant to pass her feelings on to readers. This is how we edited today's article.
> She will claim what she wrote is true, but it is often incomplete, misdirecting, or distracts from the salient points. For instance, the bit about NATO omits that Trump favors the collective defense, but with others ponying up their share of the cost. You can't suss that out from [her] article. If the writing is not going to present an accurate map, don't write it.
> I would be happy to defend every edit, but it should be obvious to the most casual observer why we did it.
> Thank you.

Take Back Your News

--

CLEVELAND (AP) — Declaring America in crisis, Donald Trump pledged to cheering Republicans and still-skeptical voters Thursday night that as president he will restore the safety they fear they're losing, strictly curb immigration and save the nation from Hillary Clinton's record of "death, destruction, terrorism and weakness."

Confidently addressing the finale of his party's less-than-smooth national convention, the ~~billionaire~~ businessman declared the nation's problems too staggering to be fixed within the confines of traditional politics.

"I have joined the political arena so that the powerful can no longer beat up on people that cannot defend themselves," Trump said.

The 71-year-old's ~~celebrity businessman's~~ acceptance of the Republican nomination caps his ~~improbable~~ takeover of the GOP, a party that plunges into the general election united in opposition to Clinton but still divided over Trump.

His address on the closing night of the convention marked his highest-profile opportunity yet to heal those divisions and show voters he's prepared for the presidency. ~~Ever the showman, he~~ He fed off the energy of the crowd, stepping back to soak in applause and joining the delegates as they chanted, "USA."

As the crowd, fiercely opposed to Clinton, broke out in its oft-used refrain of "Lock her up," he waved them off, and instead declared, "Let's defeat her in November." Yet he also accused her of "terrible, terrible crimes" and said her greatest achievement may have been staying out of prison.

He offered himself as a powerful ally of those who feel Washington has left them behind.

"I'm with you, and I will fight for you, and I will win for you," he declared.

He accused Clinton, his ~~far-more-experienced~~ Democratic rival, of utterly lacking the good judgment to serve in the White House and as the military's commander in chief.

"This is the legacy of Hillary Clinton: death, destruction, terrorism and weakness," he said. "But Hillary Clinton's legacy does not have to be America's legacy."

In a direct appeal to Americans shaken by a summer of violence at home and around the world, Trump promised that if he takes office in January, "safety will be restored."

As he moves into the general election campaign, he's sticking to the controversial proposals of his primary campaign, including building a wall along the entire U.S.-Mexico border and suspending immigration from nations "compromised by terrorism."

But in a nod to a broader swath of Americans, he said young people in predominantly black cities "have as much of a right to live out their dreams as any other child in America." He also vowed to protect gays and lesbians from violence and oppression, a pledge that was greeted with applause from the crowd.

"As a Republican, it is so nice to hear you cheering for what I just said," he responded.

Trump was introduced by his daughter Ivanka, who announced a childcare policy proposal that the campaign had not mentioned before.

"As president, my father will change the labor laws that were put in place at a time when women weren't a significant portion of the workplace, and he will focus on making quality childcare affordable and accessible for all," she said.

~~Trump took the stage in Cleveland facing a daunting array of challenges, many of his own making. Though he vanquished 16 primary rivals, he's viewed with unprecedented negativity by the broader electorate,~~

Evidence of media failure

~~and is struggling in particular with younger voters and minorities, groups GOP leaders know they need for the party to grow.~~

~~The first three days of this week's convention gathering bordered on chaos, starting with a plagiarism charge involving his wife Melania Trump's speech and moving on to Texas Sen. Ted Cruz's dramatic refusal to endorse him from the convention stage.~~

Then, Trump sparked more questions **about his Oval Office readiness** by suggesting in the midst of the convention that the U.S. might not defend America's NATO partners with him as president. The remarks, in an interview published online Wednesday by The New York Times, deviate from decades of American doctrine ~~and seem to reject the 67-year-old alliance's bedrock principle of collective defense~~.

Trump reinforced his position from the convention stage, saying the United States has been "picking up the cost" of NATO's defenses for too long. He also disavowed America's foreign policy posture under both Democrat and Republican presidents, criticizing "fifteen years of wars in the Middle East" and declaring that "Americanism, not globalism, will be our credo."

"As long as we are led by politicians who will not put 'America First,' then we can be assured that other nations will not treat America with respect," he said.

He had promised to describe "major, major" tax cuts. ~~But his economic proposals Thursday night were vague, centering on unspecified plans to create millions of jobs.~~ He promised a "simplified" tax system for the middle class and businesses, fewer regulations and renegotiation of trade deals that he says have put working class Americans at a disadvantage.

"These are the forgotten men and women of our country," he said. "People who work hard but no longer have a voice."

~~At every turn, Trump drew sharp contrasts with Clinton, casting her as both unqualified for the presidency and too tied to Washington elites to understand voters' struggles. Her greatest accomplishment, Trump said, was avoiding punishment from the FBI for her use of a private email and personal server while as secretary of state.~~

~~Indeed, Clinton was aggressively attacked throughout the four-day Republican convention, with delegates repeatedly chanting, "Lock her up."~~

Democrats will formally nominate Clinton at their convention next week in Philadelphia. Clinton was on the verge of naming a running mate to join her in taking on Trump and his vice presidential pick, Indiana Gov. Mike Pence, in the general election. Virginia Sen. Tim Kaine has emerged as her top choice.

Should a journalist be aware of and report on demeanor since reaction speaks a lot when it comes to character? Isn't some scrutiny in order since demeanor can have an impact on facts as they are presented?

Demeanor—how a person speaks—does matter. When Antony repeats that Brutus is an honorable man, he expects listeners to recognize Brutus has no honor. But reporters are not so much reporting demeanor as being confused by rhetoric.

Rhetoric is how we express what we think to others and check what others express to us. In classical times, Rhetoric was taught as invention, arrangement, style, memory, and delivery. [Unfortunately, in the 1500s, invention and arrangement—the ordering and testing of evidence—were removed leaving Rhetoric absent its honesty, to focus on presentation alone.]

Those who pay attention to speaker rhetoric need know how frequently reporters mask or warp what is said. "Belligerent" can represent the tone of the speaker or, just as easily, the opinion of the reporter.

Similarly, reporters often confuse a negotiating position with a final and agreed upon promise. "Oh, I will never settle for that" often is a statement that evaporates after an agreement is finalized.

It is silly but common for media not to distinguish between what a candidate advocates before the election, promised to work towards after the election, and ultimately delivers in office following negotiations.

Media adjectives and adverbs editorialize

Editors serve their reporters best when they rein in theatric use of adjectives and adverbs. On December 23, 2016, we emailed the wire service:

> Dear [New wire service rep],
>
> [The wire service] has been important to this country in the past and needs to be important in the future. I would appreciate the opportunity to come to New York to meet with you. Perhaps some time in January might be convenient.
>
> I can take any [wire] political story on any day and find poor journalistic habit that -- knowingly or unknowingly -- come across as judgmental carping. Just today, reading [reporter] . . .
>
> BC-US--Trump,11th Ld-Writethru
>
> Trump: US must 'greatly strengthen' nuclear capability
>
> -- White House Correspondent
>
> In graf one, was it that Trump "**abruptly** called for" or did "Trump called for"?
>
> In graf three, was it necessary to say, "his **palatial** private club" or simply "his private club"?
>
> Also in graf three, why would the judgmental [reporter] think it necessary for Trump to "say why he raised the issue on Tuesday"?
>
> In graf 10, [reporter] continues to mischaracterize Trump's opinion of Putin, "has spoken **favorably** about Putin". Favorably is ambiguous and suggests more than that Trump respects Putin's capabilities. Trump said, "I mean [Putin] has done -- whether you like him or don't like him -- he is doing a great job in rebuilding the image of Russia and also rebuilding Russia period." (2007)
>
> In graf 13, about a foolish gotcha question from a presidential debate about which leg of the nuclear triad was more important, [reporter] misjudges a Trump

Evidence of media failure

response that he chose to answer differently, pointing to proliferation as a greater problem. Either [reporter] didn't understand or didn't want to.

In graf 14, Hillary Clinton's opinion about Trump being "too erratic and unpredictable" is not context; it is simply out of date, irrelevant, and out of place.

So we have half a dozen concerns in one article, and not one editor over [reporter] has seen fit to clean up her work. Multiply this by the number of days since I started being concerned at least six months ago, before the election and the number of articles each day.

[The wire service] still is campaigning. It's why Dick Cheney said, in a candid moment during an interview, "We don't need you anymore." it is why Trump continued to bypass the MSM with his "Thank you" tour -- You can't see your habits.

Understand that I supported at least two other candidates before I resigned myself to Trump was the only candidate who recognized what the national press cannot see for itself -- that the fourth estate had been co-opted by its own opinions to become more a danger to our republic than a safeguard.

Do not make the mistake to believe that I am simply on the other side of a political divide. We both want to hone skills enough so that we can restore to rhetoric the honesty it used to have before the 1500s when the integrity of what was said mattered. I'll bet you didn't know that was when rhetoric became just salesmanship.

Media labels push a political agenda

"Conservative", "moderate", "liberal", "Republican", "Democrat", and "non-partisan" are labels applied with political intention. Reporters persistently label, emphasize labels, and define what labels mean.

"Antifa" has been described as being anti-fascist despite its fascistic tendencies, as if the common definition meant more than methods actually practiced by the group.

When it fits their preference, media will also minimize a definition as inconsequential and dismiss it.

In the *Federalist*, Stella Morabito described how media manipulated people into a "nervous breakdown" over the events in Charlottesville. VA. Setting aside, for the moment, the role of entertainment and academia, she singles out "the manipulation of our language; the deliberate use of such loaded language to cultivate extreme emotions in people, particularly anger and resentment; and the role of mass media as a nuclear device to impose those perceptions on a mass scale." [4]

---

[4] http://thefederalist.com/2017/08/25/americas-post-charlottesville-nervous-breakdown-deliberately-induced/

She says, "The whole point of manipulating language is to obfuscate in order to control." It builds to an emotional crescendo, not intellectual understanding. Coordinated mob violence has little to do with historical monuments and free speech and everything to do with indoctrination.

Shaping vocabulary shapes the mental battlefield, forging associations semantically that replace understanding with anti-intellectual programming.

Media descriptives and logical fallacies color reporting

When medieval students argued about how many angels could dance on the head of a pin, they were uninterested in either angels or the final tally. Speakers were interested in forming arguments that avoided logical fallacies and listeners were interested in detecting such fallacies by those who tried to insert them.

A recent book lists at least 42 logical fallacies worth being able to defend against.[5]

Curricula in public schools today commonly pay lip service to logical fallacies in 9th Grade, but cover just a few of them. The critical skill of cleansing rhetoric of its fleas seems of only passing interest.

On July 17, 2017, we emailed:

> Hi, [Wire Service rep] . . .
> It isn't even 9 AM on Monday and [the wire service] has mortgaged its integrity for the week.
>> The newest version attempts to attract conservative support by allowing insurers to offer **skimpy** coverage plans alongside more robust ones
>
> Where do you find your adjectives!
> Oh, and where are the editors who would try other options?
> This isn't the first time your writers have pushed this non-descriptive opinion. Are we talking about catastrophic insurance to cover just unusual and expensive diseases and injuries? Say so.
>
> ---
>
> Please stop being a shill for nameless critics throwing mud.
>> But critics have criticized Trump when he's pushed "Made in America" in the past because so many of the products he and his family members have sold over the years were manufactured overseas. That includes merchandise sold

---

[5] Perie, Madson. *How to win every argument The use and Abuse of Logic.* © 2006. Continuum International Publishing Group. New York.

Evidence of media failure

under his own name and his eldest daughter's, including clothing items and shoes.

Is [the wire service] so obtuse that it swallows the "either/or" logical fallacy of bifurcation?

I hope not.

I despair that [the wire service] will ever learn, or even cares to do so. Perhaps rather than correcting [wire service] articles we should add at the end what it is that [the wire service] tried to do so that readers will understand what they would have been fed.

Imagine if we added:

> The [wire service] called the proposed coverage 'skimpy' when in fact it was designed specifically to cover severe and high cost health problems that could otherwise bankrupt subscribers. We have corrected the error and apologize for our wire service.

Or we could say:

> The [wire service] mistakenly fed readers the Bifurcation Fallacy — presenting only two alternatives when others exist. [The wire service] essentially tells readers Trump meant that all manufacturing had to be done in the United States or abroad when readers know that is obviously not the case. . We have corrected the error and apologize for our wire service.

Thank you.

Media manufacture messages

Media habitually insinuates itself between readers and news to interpret what happened rather than describe what happened. They too often misrepresent what was said to substitute a selective distillation of what they believe was said. Reporting that so-and-so talked about something suppresses what was actually discussed.

On July 1, 2016, the *Rome Sentinel* editorial reflected to readers of concerns about the quality of journalism they read and view:

> **Headline**: Thoughts on reporting America First
>
> Americans are smart enough to recognize that internationalist Donald Trump's desire to work for America first is far different from Charles Lindbergh pushing "America First" isolationism 75 years ago before World War II.
>
> Americans are smart enough, then, to recognize it is politics, not news, when national news outlets like CNN, Time, and our own wire service, the Associated Press, push Lindbergh and Trump comparisons without giving you the transcript of Trump's foreign policy speech to decide for yourself. The [Wire Service] did not link to Trump's speech but you can read it at: http://ow.ly/iRfU301PIEq
>
> No wonder public respect for national news media is plummeting even lower than that of Congress.
>
> Politicians play to a generation of voters who were drilled in school to trust "experts" with credentials instead of those whose expertise comes from explaining things so clearly that even we can understand. Politicians play to national news outlet reporters who were schooled to be more malleable to political demagoguery.

Take Back Your News

This is the generation of national news reporters who, to elect Obama, created the "Journolist"— a subversive email exchange that mistook reporting for an opportunity to foster political change. They believed they were hired to change the world instead of report the news.

News is more than information. "News" is information put in context that you need to know to more accurately plan your future. "Information" may be true, but it is not always news and often becomes noise. When national news outlets push Charles Lindbergh's isolationism, the information becomes noise. They jam the limited bandwidth you need to help you differentiate between competing candidates for President.

They will claim their information is true, but their words are weapons to shape the political battlefield. The jury is still out whether the Associated Press and other national news outlets are either ignorant of the difference between news and noise, or actively pushing you toward their particular politics.

Either way, you are going to have to become the expert at choosing experts who focus on what matters and who give you evidence to back up their claims. If you read the transcript of Trump's foreign policy speech, you will arm yourself to decide about Trump, to defend against major news outlets, and to choose which "experts" to trust.

Our wire service objected to publishing the editorial, suggesting there might have been a licensing issue as to why a transcript was not linked. Not likely:

> I was sorry to run it, too, but my responsibility to the readers is to show them how they can be driven to a mistaken conclusion.
>
> If [the wire service] believes that the significant point is a rights issue, [the wire service leaves itself] open for narrative manipulation: Trump = isolationist. A reading of the speech does not suggest that.
> - Where along the continuum between globalist and isolationist would Trump fit?
> - What kind of special deals are allowed to be baked into ostensibly globalist treaties?
>
> There is an opportunity for journalism to be found if people will not willfully overlook it.

Our back and forth with the wire service extended to other campaign issues, including their artificial noise about twitter graphics, Clinton campaign emails, following the Astroturf trail, and promoting messages from campaign shills and outright propagandists at face value without explaining background and context.

Quoting a party shill without qualification is worse than speculation; it is malfeasance. Mainstream media too often serves as a megaphone for unexamined unverified spin.

Evidence of media failure

Media plant Improvised Editorial Devices (IEDs)

Improvised Editorial Devices (IEDs) — words, verb choices, subsidiary clauses, unverified spin — are as deadly to reader understanding as Improvised Explosive Devices (IEDs) have been deadly to soldiers in Iraq.

Our editors root out IEDs buried in news feeds so readers have the opportunity to make their own decisions.

Operationally, editors duplicate original wire service political articles so editors can edit a clean copy before it is run in the newspaper. Other editors are welcome to compare the originals with the edited versions. We regularly email wire service officials of our concerns. Here is an early example:

> Hi, [Wire service standards editor] . . .
> Congratulations. [our bureau chief] says you are our new Standards Editor.
> Let me introduce myself. I am the fifth generation of our family to publish the 10K circulation Rome (NY) *Daily Sentinel*, where I have worked for the last 42 years.
> I am unfamiliar with your position, but [reference], formerly of [news publication], had commented to someone else,
>> "..., instead of ranting on Facebook, why not write a nice, calm, and convincing letter to [name], their Standards Editor?"

That was in response to a blog comment of ours that said:

> I had to offer the newsroom corrective suggestions when the article failed to note until the seventh graf that the man shot by police [in Milwaukee] was armed.
> I said to the newsroom in no uncertain terms that I expect them to edit [wire] stories to remove all IEDs -- Improvised Editing Devices -- before publication.
> ...

As I emailed the bloggers [and to the standards editor]:

> - When [the wire service] buries in the 7th graf that the Wisconsin man killed by police was armed and waiving a gun, that is an IED -- an Improvised Editing Device -- that does the reader a disservice.
> - When [it] tucks unsubstantiated claims in articles, that is an IED.
> - When [it] uses charged adjectives in articles, that is an IED.
>
> Since I now know that [it] has a standards editor, and because I am interested in top quality [wire service] reporting, I am enclosing today's episode below.
> Thank you for being there. Good luck!

Media confuse readers with jargon

Memes, narratives, code words, and dog whistles clutter reporting. Keep it simple. State the facts. Avoid innuendo. The next email describes an article dripping with reportorial condescension passed off as news. It simply doesn't sell.

What Washington inside baseball calls a "cut" isn't a cut in spending at all but rather a reduction in an expected increase.

Hi, [wire service rep] . . .

At a meeting with managers this morning I mentioned I was editing yet another [wire service] article [see below] to remove the unnecessary noise. Two editors at the meeting nodded in agreement, saying that both in news and sports heavy editing had become more necessary, particularly in cutlines because of shoddy workmanship.

I thought the unsolicited corroboration was worth passing on to you and your editors.

I have included today's work for your editors' edification and education.

Thank you.

Trump meeting with G-7 leaders after going on offensive

TAORMINA, Italy (AP) — In the Middle East, President Donald Trump [Note: Get to the meat. Avoid conjecture and opinion.] was feted with pageantry, the leaders of Saudi Arabia and Israel seemingly in competition to outdo the other with the warmth of their welcomes and the depth of their pledges of cooperation.

[Note: No reason to inject opinion when the reporters could have used the space to report.] But in Europe, Trump has faced a far cooler reception and has been eager to go on the offensive.

[Note: "Cajoled"? Really? "Scolding"? Really? Juxtaposing Article V with 9/11 without explaining the concerns hoe Article V might be misused? Really?] Cajoled on issues like climate change and NATO's defense pact, he's responded by scolding some of the United States' most loyal allies for not paying their fair share. He's also refused to explicitly back the mutual defense agreement that has been activated only once, during the darkest hours of September 2001.

And now Trump is at the final stop of his maiden international trip, a [Note: Grueling for reporters or for Trump?] grueling nine-day, five-stop marathon. He will remain in Europe for the The journey's last two days, this time in will be spent at a picturesque coastal town in Sicily for a gathering of the G-7.

[Note: "warily"? Also, [the wire service] continues to interpret for itself that "America First" means isolationism when evidence has clearly shown Trump's policy favors international cooperation and involvement that advances the interests of American citizens. That is certainly not "disentangling." This trip's meetings on terrorism hardly can be considered disentangling.] Once more, he will likely be received warily, a president who ran on a campaign of "America First" with suggestions of disentangling the United States from international pacts, now engaged in two days of pomp and policy Trump will meet with the leaders of the United Kingdom, France, Germany, Italy, Japan and Canada.

"There is no doubt that this will be the most challenging G-7 summit in years," said Donald Tusk, president of the European Council.

He said the group's leaders "sometimes have very different views" on topics such as climate change and trade, "but our role as the EU is to do everything to

Evidence of media failure

maintain the unity of the G-7 on all fronts. Most importantly unity needs to be maintained when it comes to defending rule-based international order."

The White House believes that Trump has made personal breakthroughs with his peers, having now met one-on-one with all the leaders of G-7.

"It's time for him to have an intimate discussion and understand their issues but, more importantly, for them to understand our issues," national economic adviser Gary Cohn told reporters on Air Force One late Thursday.

One of those relationships was on display as Trump began the day with a meeting with Japanese Prime Minister Shinzo Abe. The president hosted Abe at the White House and his Mar-a-Lago resort back in February, where they appeared to hit it off.

Abe was the latest world leader to publicly flatter Trump, saluting his visit to the Middle East and address to NATO on Thursday.

[Note: Unnecessary and out of place attempt to suggest lack of seriousness. "Unfortunately," Abe told reporters, "this time around we won't be able to play golf together."

The president said he and Abe would cover many topics, including North Korea, which he said "is very much on our minds."

"It's a big problem, it's a world problem, but it will be solved at some point. It will be solved, [Note: An unnecessary addition put in to poke fun of Trump's speaking style] you can bet on that," Trump said. North Korea has conducted a series of recent missile tests, rattling its Pacific neighbors.

Foreign policy will be the focus on Friday, with meetings on Syria, Libya, North Korea, Afghanistan and Pakistan. Other meetings over the two days will include discussions of global economy and climate, a meeting with small African nations — Trump will be seated between the leaders of Niger and Tunisia — and migration issues.

Trade will also be a big topic, with Cohn saying the United States' guiding principle will be "we will treat you the way you treat us," suggesting that retaliatory tariffs could be imposed.

The day will feature a welcoming ceremony and concert at the remains of an ancient Greek temple, as well as a relentless number of meetings[Note: Really? Fact based? And what does "attention" mean? Scott Adams has written how what appears to be lack of attention often means high focus on substance.], many of which White House aides are hoping to keep short in order to keep Trump's attention. What the Sicily stay will likely not offer: a news conference, as Trump appears set to defy presidential tradition and not hold one during the entire trip.

The Republican president arrived in Italy fresh off delivering [Note: "rebuke"? Really? "personal"? Really? Are you sure that it wasn't a necessary statement of fact of obvious interest to American taxpayers?] an unprecedented, personal rebuke to NATO, traveling to its gleaming new Brussels headquarters to lecture its leaders to their faces on the members the message they need for them to live up to the NATO requirement to spend more 2 percent of their gross domestic product on defense.

"This is not fair to the people and taxpayers of the United States," Trump said. "If NATO countries made their full and complete contributions, then NATO would be even stronger than it is today, especially from the threat of terrorism."

The 28-member nations, plus soon-to-join Montenegro, will renew an old vow to move toward spending 2 percent of their gross domestic product on defense by 2024. Only five members meet the target: Britain, Estonia, debt-

Take Back Your News

laden Greece, Poland and the United States, which spends more on defense than all the other allies combined.

Trump refused to say he would adhere to the mutual defense pact, known as Article V, though the White House later claimed that his very presence alongside twisted World Trade Center steel — a memorial outside NATO headquarters — was evidence enough of his commitment.

"~~I think it's a bit silly because by being here at such a ceremony, we all understand that by being part of NATO we treat the obligations and commitments," said press~~ Press secretary Sean Spicer, who dubbed speculation about Trump's intent "laughable."

[Note: News? Or catty gossip? Does this tell me what I need to know as a reader or does it simply reinforce your perceptions of Trump? All of what follows appears more like guerilla warfare against someone who had pointed out your propensity for guerilla warfare. Trump is not against journalism. He is against what has been passed off as journalism by people who should know better.]~~As Trump spoke, the NATO leaders, including German Chancellor Angela Merkel and French President Emmanuel Marcon, stood in awkward silence. Later, as they took the traditional "family photo" group shot, the heads of state quietly kept their distance from Trump, who minutes earlier was caught on video appearing to push the prime minister of Montenegro out of the way to get to his spot.~~

~~The president's remarkable public scolding of NATO came amid a backdrop of uncertainty in Brussels toward Trump over his past comments publicly cheering the United Kingdom's vote to leave the EU last summer and slamming the alliance during his transition as "a vehicle for Germany."~~

~~But while Trump lectured some of the United States' strongest allies, he cozied up to the repressive regime in Saudi Arabia while pushing for the Arab world to root out extremism at home. He made deals for more than $100 billion in military equipment, christened a hurriedly-finished counter-terrorism center, and was the guest of honor at a number of lavish welcoming ceremonies, one complete with a sword dance.~~

~~It was a similar story in Israel, where Prime Minister Benjamin Netanyahu warmly greeted Trump and the president reciprocated with emotional appearances at the Western Wall and Holocaust museum and suggested that there was an opening for peace with the Palestinians.~~

--

What we ran in its place:

Trump meeting with G-7 leaders

TAORMINA, Italy — President Donald Trump is at the final stop of his maiden international trip, a nine-day, five-stop marathon. The journey's last two days will be spent at a picturesque coastal town in Sicily for a gathering of the G-7.

Trump will meet with the leaders of the United Kingdom, France, Germany, Italy, Japan and Canada.

"There is no doubt that this will be the most challenging G-7 summit in years," said Donald Tusk, president of the European Council.

He said the group's leaders "sometimes have very different views" on topics such as climate change and trade, "but our role as the EU is to do everything to maintain the unity of the G-7 on all fronts. Most importantly unity needs to be maintained when it comes to defending rule-based international order."

The White House believes that Trump has made personal breakthroughs with his peers, having now met one-on-one with all the leaders of G-7.

Evidence of media failure

"It's time for him to have an intimate discussion and understand their issues but, more importantly, for them to understand our issues," national economic adviser Gary Cohn told reporters on Air Force One late Thursday.

One of those relationships was on display as Trump began the day with a meeting with Japanese Prime Minister Shinzo Abe. The president hosted Abe at the White House and his Mar-a-Lago resort back in February.

Abe was the latest world leader to publicly flatter Trump, saluting his visit to the Middle East and address to NATO on Thursday.

The president said he and Abe would cover many topics, including North Korea, which he said "is very much on our minds."

"It's a big problem, it's a world problem, but it will be solved at some point," Trump said. North Korea has conducted a series of recent missile tests, rattling its Pacific neighbors.

Foreign policy will be the focus on Friday, with meetings on Syria, Libya, North Korea, Afghanistan and Pakistan. Other meetings over the two days will include discussions of global economy and climate, a meeting with small African nations — Trump will be seated between the leaders of Niger and Tunisia — and migration issues.

Trade will also be a big topic, with Cohn saying the United States' guiding principle will be "we will treat you the way you treat us," suggesting that retaliatory tariffs could be imposed.

The day will feature a welcoming ceremony and concert at the remains of an ancient Greek temple, as well as a number of meetings.

The Republican president arrived in Italy fresh off delivering NATO members the message they need to live up to the NATO requirement to spend 2 percent of gross domestic product on defense.

"This is not fair to the people and taxpayers of the United States," Trump said. "If NATO countries made their full and complete contributions, then NATO would be even stronger than it is today, especially from the threat of terrorism."

Only five members meet the target: Britain, Estonia, debt-laden Greece, Poland and the United States, which spends more on defense than all the other allies combined.

Trump refused to say he would adhere to the mutual defense pact, known as Article V, though the White House claimed that his very presence alongside twisted World Trade Center steel — a memorial outside NATO headquarters — was evidence enough of his commitment.

Press secretary Sean Spicer, who dubbed speculation about Trump's intent "laughable."

The wire service replied that they would share what is meant by cuts with budget reporters. Of course they already know. Their reply is classic passive aggressive.

Media postmodernize word meanings

Loaded words at least bear a resemblance to traditional word meanings. Present-day postmodernists hijack words to mean whatever they say they mean. They apply the Lewis Carroll approach to words: Humpty Dumpty explains to Alice that words mean what he says they mean and nothing more.

Postmodern battle tactics allow them to redefine words to mean something other than meanings conventionally used and not explain their new meanings.

Words are powerful tools to be used or misused. Duplicitous politicians expect citizens to assume their words operate under commonly accepted definitions. Their hope is that citizens will discover too late that something quite different is what was meant.

Those in favor of the common definition of *democracy* would be surprised that some politicians would pervert the word to allow a majority voting to validate mob rule that civil society would not tolerate.

Postmodernists believe it's quite all right to lie to support their positions — as several current and past public officials readily admit.[6]

Generations of postmodern schooling have nudged many graduates who have become journalists to believe that ends justify the means. As a result, they feel it's quite okay to misrepresent ideas. Postmodern pseudo-journalists regularly fail to challenge politicians who say silly things.

Postmodernism is a destroyer, not a builder and a permutation of Machiavellian power politics:

1) Whomever is in power gets to set the rules, and
2) Whatever gets one power becomes a working rule whether or not the practice was agreed upon beforehand.

Postmodern political practice has insinuated itself into mainstream media in such a way reporters will violate journalism to get their point across. How ironic that pseudo-journalists represent themselves as arbiters of what news is real or fake.

When the media does not police itself, individuals must shoulder responsibility to judge the integrity of news as read. We emailed our wire service:

> [The wire service] has the persistent habit — which it denies all the time — of inserting clauses of nasty innuendo, unnecessary and ill-placed repetitions, and demeaning adjectives.

---

[6] Among them Cass Sunstein and Robert Reich.

Evidence of media failure

> [The wire service] — along with the other media regularly called out — chooses not to recognize that journalism can only be earned one story at a time.
>
> Like the others, [the wire service] tries to shield itself from deserved criticism by wrapping itself in the First Amendment when it knows full well that "the enemy" applies not to all press, but instances of failure to provide a decent representation of what happened.

Later we warned them:

> [The wire service] is on track to have more members resign as they realize [the wire service] wants to make readers' decisions for them, rather than help improve the accuracy of their mental map of reality so they can make their own decisions as they plan their better future.
>
> [The wire service] fails to understand that as people learn more about post-modern warfare of ideas, a misrepresentation is a lie. After a single lie, people can never be trusted again. Any decent newspaper publisher knows trust is the only thing we have to sell.
>
> ...

Evidence: Media sell opinion as news

All writers of fiction, history, and news choose content, words, and presentation. For news, judicious choice of words, phrases, and facts should most accurately represent what happened.

It's possible to write absent facts and possible to insert irrelevant facts. Good reporting selects salient facts, leaving out the rest.

The wire service started sending what it labels "analysis" that appears to be an opportunity for a reporter to push personal editorial opinion as fact.

On October 3, 2016 we emailed to our wire service rep:

> Are stories submitted by [wire service] reporters edited before release?
>
> In the [wire] story today on Trump taxes, were we to run it, I would cut 22 paragraphs of opinion and insert one sentence of fact:
>
>> NEW YORK (AP) — Ever defiant, Donald Trump and his Republican allies largely embraced a report that said the New York businessman may not have paid federal income taxes for nearly two decades after he and his companies lost nearly $916 million in a single year.

Take Back Your News

[Sentence added:] *What Trump did was legal and others, including Hillary Clinton and the New York Times that broke the story, have avoided taxes using similar opportunities in the Tax Code.*

In a story published online late Saturday, The Times said it anonymously received the first pages of Trump's 1995 state income tax filings in New York, New Jersey and Connecticut. The filings show a net loss of $915,729,293 in federal taxable income for the year.

His campaign said that Trump had paid "hundreds of millions" of dollars in other kinds of taxes over the years.

Trump has refused to release his tax returns, breaking with four decades of presidential campaign tradition.

Similar to what happens with "analyses" the media will push polls as somehow authoritative despite questionable polling technique. Often the selection of respondents is at odds with reality. At other times "push poll" questions direct respondents toward preferred answers. Polls skew reporting simply by stressing opinion as fact. We passed a warning to readers through Facebook, Twitter and blogs:

> Ask all that you know to send back to their local newspapers wire service copy that contains opinion, conjecture, extraneous "facts" and selective reporting. Demand local editors correct misrepresentations before publishing dreck verbatim that is a disservice to their readers.
>
> A Shakespearian style Helen Hayes 1956 radio show had a remark I will purloin and apply to Wire Service reporters:
>
>> Journalist hacks "spread compost on weeds."

By email we sent the wire service the edited copy below.

Dear [Bureau chief]

Is it impossible for [wire service] reporters to exclude opinion and conjecture?

And can they order a story, focusing on what matters?

New York Newspaper Publishers sent a reminder to member publishers to be sure to edit wire service copy for quality.

Please forward the latest suggested revisions to the appropriate people. ...

Headline: Presidential debate emphasizes choice for future of the nation

WASHINGTON — ~~His presidential campaign in peril,~~ [Flaw: unsubstantiated editorial opinion does not belong here, particularly as the lead.] ~~Donald Trump left no doubt he'll spend the final weeks before the election dredging up decades-old sexual allegations against Hillary Clinton's husband,~~ [Flaw: More unsubstantiated conjecture, particularly odious since it was decades-old conversation dredged up by his opposition.] ~~even if it turns off voters whose support he desperately needs.~~ [Flaw: Still more conjecture. Stick to reporting.]

Hillary Clinton and Donald Trump met Sunday night for the second presidential debate.

Evidence of media failure

The debate was the culmination of a weekend that began with the release of a video in which Trump is heard describing attempts to have consensual sex with a married woman. The businessman said he wasn't proud of his comments and insisted he had "great respect for women."[Added and moved up from below.]

Questioned ~~at Sunday's debate~~ early about ~~his~~ vulgar remarks about women, Trump accused Bill Clinton of having been "abusive to women" and said Hillary Clinton attacked those women "viciously." He declared the Democratic nominee had "tremendous hate in her heart."

~~Clinton tried at times to take the high road, glossing over Trump's charges and accusing him of trying to distract from his political troubles. "Anything to avoid talking about your campaign and the way it's exploding," she said.~~ [Flaw: Premise of "high road" not supported by evidence presented.]

~~Indeed, Trump entered Sunday night's debate facing enormous pressure from the Republican Party and even his own running mate, Indiana Gov. Mike Pence. Numerous~~ Some Washington beltway Republicans revoked their support for Trump following the release of a 2005 video in which he is heard bragging about how his fame allowed him to "do anything" to women. [Added useful context:] The video offered nothing that hadn't been covered years ago in Trump's autobiography. Trump's remarks were similar to those attributed to Bill Clinton by golfing partner Vernon Jordan.

~~House~~ GOP ~~lawmakers were expected to address Trump's campaign in a rare, out-of-session conference call Monday morning. Hours before the meeting,~~ Pence urged Republicans to stand behind Trump. "This is a choice between two futures," he said on "Fox News."

~~For voters appalled by Trump's words, the businessman likely did little to ease their concerns. He~~ Trump denied he had kissed and groped women without their consent, dismissing his comments as "locker room" talk.

But Trump's intensely loyal supporters were likely to be energized by his vigorous criticism of Clinton. He labeled her "the devil" and ~~promised~~ quipped she would "be in jail" if he were president because of her email practices at the State Department — a threat that drew widespread criticism.

"That was a quip," Kellyanne Conway, Trump's campaign manager, said Monday on MSNBC's "Morning Joe." She also wouldn't confirm Trump's plans, announced at the debate, to appoint a special prosecutor to investigate Clinton if he is victorious. ~~Trump was "channeling the frustration" of voters, she said.~~

~~The debate was the culmination of a stunning stretch in the race for the White House, which began with the surprise release of the video in which Trump is heard describing attempts to have sex with a married woman. The businessman said he wasn't proud of his comments and insisted he had "great respect for women."~~

~~The tension between Trump and Clinton was palpable from the start of their 90-minute debate, the second time they have faced off in the presidential campaign. They did not shake hands as they met at center stage.~~

~~Trump, who is several inches taller than Clinton, stood close behind her as she answered questions from voters. At other times, he paced the stage, repeatedly interrupting her and criticizing the moderators.~~

In a ~~brazen~~ pre-debate move, Trump met with three women who accused the former president of sexual harassment and even rape, then invited them to sit in the debate hall, not far from Bill Clinton and his family. The former president never faced any criminal charges over the allegations, and a lawsuit over an alleged rape was dismissed. He settled a lawsuit [Note: Check documents to see

35

Take Back Your News

if the $800,000 is accurate. If so, include.]with one of the women who claimed harassment.

Trump ~~struggled at times to articulate detailed policy proposals, repeatedly dancing around~~ did not give detailed answers to questions about how he would fulfill his vow replace President Barack Obama's health care law.

~~Breaking with his running mate,~~ Trump made clear he did not agree with Pence on how to deal with war-torn Syria. Last week, Pence said the U.S. military should be ready to strike Syrian military targets are President Bashar Assad's command. The threat was a departure from Trump's focus on hitting Islamic State targets. Said Trump, "He and I haven't spoken and I disagree."

~~Trump's campaign was already struggling before the new video was released, due in part to his uneven performance in the first presidential debate.~~ [Flaw: Opinion.]~~Many Republicans saw Sunday's showdown as his last best chance to salvage his campaign.~~ [Flaw: Conjecture.]

The Trump video overshadowed potentially damaging revelations about Clinton's paid speeches to Wall Street firms. Emails released by WikiLeaks last week showed Clinton told a group that it's acceptable for a president to project differing positions in public and private. [Note: Place this relevant news higher in the article. The dated video tends to obscure this substantive news.]

~~Asked if that's "two-faced," Clinton pointed to Abraham Lincoln's effort to get the 13th Amendment passed, allowing emancipation of slaves, by lawmakers who did not support African-American equality.~~

"I was making the point it is hard sometimes to get the Congress to do what you want them to do. ~~That was a great display of presidential leadership.~~"

~~Rolling his eyes,~~ Trump said, ~~"Now she's blaming the late, great Abraham Lincoln."~~

In the debate's final moments, the candidates briefly put aside their animosity when asked by a voter if they respected anything about each other.

Clinton said she respected Trump's children, calling them "incredibly able and devoted."

Trump, as if pulling a line directly from the Clinton campaign, called his Democratic opponent a "fighter."

"She doesn't quit, she doesn't give up," he said. "I respect that."

Opinion is not news. Newsreaders and commentators should not second guess those in the news:
- "He should have said…"
- "His tone turned people off/on…"
- "He would connect better if he …"

Media equivocate to register opinion

Reporters will assume facts not in evidence.

They will claim, for instance, that while options are being considered, "no plans" exist to describe military options. The statement suggests planners are unprepared rather than that plans have not been released. They did not care that Trump explained he would not telegraph to others what his plans are.

Evidence of media failure

The wire service that reported no plans exist dissembles in a manner purposely constructed to misrepresent the case. The wire service could write clearly and succinctly but chose not to do so.

Media push emotional opinion

High dudgeon is seldom called for in real journalism. Many in the mainstream media, especially talking heads, have decided that emotion makes them seem caring and real.

Not really. It makes them seem incapable of reporting.

On Aug. 14, 2017, we emailed:

> Subject: One-sided opinion is not news
> Dear [Wire service rep] . . .
> In [a wire] "analysis" — really an editorial and not news — [the reporter] wrote:
>> WASHINGTON — Why doesn't President Donald Trump just unequivocally condemn white supremacists?
>
> It could just as easily have been written:
>> WASHINGTON — Why doesn't President Donald Trump just unequivocally condemn anti-fa, free speech opponents, or anarchy-fascists?
>
> We don't know who started the violence in Charlottesville. Why would [the reporter] not want the others condemned?
>
> We will know, after a DOJ investigation into civil rights violations, who packed the people in, who arranged the traffic, and how the civil police presence was handled.
>
> But [the wire service], and [the reporter] in particular, seems more interested in pet narratives. More than that, [the reporter], to the detriment of [the wire service's] brand, tweets to fan the flames.
>> [Screenshots of example tweets]
>
> As I have perhaps mentioned before, the Air Force would change commanders every two or three years when the B-52 squadron and Refueling Wing were located here lest one commander become too complacent and stuck in convention that might be dangerous to mission readiness.
>
> Too many newspapers across the country will run this opinion as news.
>
> Perhaps it is time to rotate [the reporter].
> Thank you.

Take Back Your News

Media speculate, project and guess

Media too readily jump to conclusions, especially conclusions that feed preconceived notions. They speculated that a draft letter by President Trump was an attempt to squelch investigation into the Trump campaign's pre-election activities. Their insinuation reflects a narrative proposed the day FBI Director James Comey was fired that presumes obstruction.

Comey's firing wouldn't be obstruction because, absent Comey, investigative work still would continue with staff. Anticipating what will be done is a guess, not news. To use the sports metaphor, that is why they play the game.

On April 3, 2017, we emailed the wire service:

Hi, [Wire service representative] . . .

[Wire service] reporters must be prescient, reporting as fact their opinions.

[The wire service wrote:
BC-US--Senate-Supreme Court
Senate panel to vote on Trump's Supreme Court nominee
WASHINGTON — A Senate panel is opening a weeklong partisan showdown over President Donald Trump's Supreme Court nominee. [Note: News reports indicate at least three Democrats indicate they will vote against a filibuster. It may happen, but is this "steadily amassing?" Did not realize the AP reporter and editor were so prescient.]

The Republican-led Judiciary Committee meets Monday and is expected to back Gorsuch and send his nomination to the full Senate, most likely on a near-party line vote. [Note: funny AP doesn't indicate that DEMOCRATS might be the reason why the change might have to be considered or say that DEMOCRAT Harry Reid changed the rules for lower court judges.] Intent on getting Trump's pick on the high court, Majority Leader Mitch McConnell of Kentucky is likely to change Senate rules so that Gorsuch can be confirmed with a simple majority in the 100-seat chamber, instead of the 60-voter threshold.

--

What we ran:

WASHINGTON — The Senate Judiciary Committee is likely to vote on President Donald Trump's Supreme Court nominee Neil Gorsuch today.

The committee meets this morning and is expected to back Gorsuch and send his nomination to the full Senate, most likely on a near-party line vote. Senate Majority Leader Mitch McConnell of Kentucky insists Gorsuch will pass a vote in the full Senate. That vote is likely to occur Friday.

Democrats will have to decide whether or not to filibuster the nomination. If they do, it would take 60 votes or a change in the rules to move the nomination to the floor where 51 votes would approve the nominee.

If Democrats filibuster, McConnell has the option to do what Democrat Harry Reid, the former Senate majority leader, did when he changed rules to

Evidence of media failure

reduce to a simple majority the number of votes to move lower court judges to a vote of the full Senate.
Thank you.

The wire service representative disagreed with the interpretation since they had been speaking with senators and staff and basing their vote count on "likely" votes. They were, they said, not prescient but basing assessments on shoe-leather reporting.

Media push unsubstantiated accusations

Sometimes there is no there there. During a media frenzy, reporters will report what other reporters are reporting simply because other reporters report it.

It's as if repeating previous misreporting from other media would validate misinformation.

On July 18, 2017, we wrote the wire service:

Hi, [wire service rep] . . .
[The wire service] and the MSM have jumped the shark.

There were 80 people at the dinner. Pictures on twitter show dozens of people. The press was there. Photographers were there.

And yet [the wire service] writes an article where none is needed. [It] writes in a stilted style to avoid saying there is no there there.

WASHINGTON — President Donald Trump had another, previously undisclosed conversation with Russian President Vladimir Putin at a summit in Germany this month.

White House spokesman Sean Spicer and National Security Council spokesman Michael Anton confirmed that Trump and Putin spoke at a dinner for world leaders and their spouses at the Group of 20 summit in Hamburg, Germany.

The conversation came hours after Trump and Putin's first official face-to-face meeting on July 7, which was originally scheduled to last just half an hour but stretched on for more than two. The two world leaders were also captured on video shaking hands and exchanging a few words after they arrived at the G-20 summit of industrialized and developing nations earlier that day.

Anton would not specify the duration of the conversation. But he said the discussion was casual and should not be characterized as a "meeting" or even a less formal, but official, "pull-aside."

Trump is right: SAD!

[The wire service] has yet to say that talking to Russians is not a crime. Collusion is not a crime. Hillary engaged in more, including the transfer of hundreds of thousands of dollars.

I am going to start writing editorials describing [the wire service's] coverage, apologizing for it, or maybe even laughing at you.

Thank you.

A wire service rep replied that he was going to draw the line because my emails were not constructive. We replied:

Dear [rep]:

> On Jul 19, 2017, at 12:22 AM, [Wire service rep] wrote
> I'm going to draw the line at this point.

No, [wire service rep], I am going to draw the line.

I am being constructive, [wire service] is not.

Look at the pictures, there are 80 guests and the press. "Previously undisclosed" breathlessly insinuates underhandedness. What for? Why? What evidence have you?

There was more evidence in Obama whispering to Putin on camera that he would have greater flexibility, and [the wire service] appears not to give a damn. Nor does [the wire service] give a damn about the greater evidence of collusion between Hillary's State Department and Russia, Hillary and the Ukraine, Hillary and the press, and -- more insidious -- members of the government leaking highly secure conversations to the detriment of the country and the press.

This would be nothing if the NYtimes did not want to manufacture something. And [the wire service] carried the NYTimes's water, perhaps because it was unthinking or lazy.

What gets reported matters. How it is reported matters. The NYTimes, and too often [the wire service], does readers a disservice by how they report and tweet -- and little if anything has changed.

If [the wire service] were honestly interested in informing readers it would spend its precious bandwidth:

* Tracking foot dragging on high level appointments and delay tactics
* Detailing the stalling tactics Democrats have used to gum up government
• Trying to explain what it is that Democrats stand for in policy other than platitudes.
• Asked Democrats what they consider the failures of Obamacare and how they should be fixed.
• Called Democrats to account for their abysmal track record for the policies they have passed.
• Pursuing the corruption evident in the previous administration's politicization of various departments of justice
• Demanded answers from Schumer about what the previous administration did and, through its appointments, continues to do -- with the same alacrity as it pursues Republicans

Evidence of media failure

> • Raising concerns about leaking to the press that suggest national security has gone rogue.
> * Pursued the DNC's reluctance to allow proper FBI investigation, instead, calling on its own to "investigate"
> * Pointing out how the MSM has overreached its job to become part of the problem, not the solution.
> • And, frankly, never explained how what Trump's team has done has been an any way illegal and never compared it to what Hillary and her team did as Secretary of State.

It has reached the point where one has to reluctantly wonder if there isn't a #dishonestPress at work. Meanwhile, [the wire service] is basically blind to its own faults, shows no remorse, and tweets out sarcastic crap.

[The wire service] does not realize that it is nothing special. Reporters are nothing special. They are only as good as their work.

And there is plenty enough substance in what I have written to [the wire service] for [the wire service] to recognize and admit there is more than a little truth to what I write.

No, [wire service rep], I am drawing the line. It is time for [the wire service] to get serious and pay attention. I want [the wire service] to succeed but [the wire service] keeps getting in its own way:

> * [The wire service] has to stop injecting editorial opinion as adjectives (like "skimpy") in place of writing the facts : Explain the difference between health insurance and healthcare. Explain the difference in personal costs between catastrophic care versus total coverage. Stop describing the CBO as "non-partisan" and explain how the CBO was gamed by Obama to seem affordable because it pushed taxes beyond the 10 year window. Explain that the CBO ranking misstates the drop-out rate by not describing those who have dropped out of Obamacare.
> * [The wire service] has to stop falling for -- and perpetrating -- logical fallacies. It sends the message that you don't respect or value your readers. In the last note I mentioned the overly-simplistic either/or bifurcation fallacy that tried to paint Trump as believing all manufacturing had to take place in the United States. That is patently at odds with Trump's reality that favoring American manufacturing makes economic sense and still engages the world economy. Use of the bifurcation fallacy makes AP sound stupid.

Thank you.

The [wire service rep] replied:

Good morning. I have no issues with substantive, editorial comments or concerns. Like the note you just wrote. But your note of last night spoke of laughing at [wire service] reporters and you made a threat about writing editorials.

To which I replied on July 19, 2017:

Hi, [Wire service rep] . . .

I have an obligation to point out to our readers if and where there is a persistent problem with what we report and editorials are the proper place for me to do that.

For the most part -- I can think of one instance some time ago -- when I actually did call the MSM, including [the wire service], to task for its reporting.

Therefore, it is no threat, it is a fact, that I will explain to readers my concerns so that readers can judge for themselves.

--

For dialog to be constructive it has to be more than dialog. Words passing each other in the night is not useful conversation. When I manage staff, I expect them to be coachable. When they are not, we have two problems: 1) the problem, and 2) the problem of dealing with the problem. When that happens, I say, "We have two problems to deal with, which do you want to deal with first?"

I have pointed out to you that [the wire service] has two problems. We'll see what happens next. [The wire service] is further back on the road to comeuppance than CNN, NYTimes, or WaPo, but [the wire service], still on that road, neither recognizes it nor, from my view, yet appears to care.

I'm done for today. We will not run the Trump dessert conversation that never should have been sent to us. [The wire service] would better spend reporter time pulling the loose threads from my off-the-top-of-my-head list.

--

My son's best baseball coach was constantly chiding the players. Some of the comments were useful. Some were noise. Players had to sort out which. My son loved and respected him. He understood that when the coach shut down on a kid, the kid was not coachable.

That's Confucius: It's wrong not to speak to someone who will listen. It's wrong to waste words on someone who will not hear.

Thank you.

Media let personal views interfere

Sometimes reporters become so alienated by subjects they are obliged to report on that they will take action to retaliate.

In one case, as Trump viewed an eclipse, he feigned to the audience that he looked directly at the sun. Since Trump was not blinded by sunlight, he obviously did not look directly at the sun. Nevertheless, many reporters chose misrepresent the case to readers to lash back at Trump.

Evidence of media failure

On August 21, 2017, we emailed:

> Dear [wire service rep] . . .
>
> You have been had.
>
> At the White House, despite all the warnings from experts about the risk of eye damage, President Donald Trump took off his eclipse glasses and looked directly at the sun.
>
> Look at the video. He played the audience and [the wire service] bit.
>
> It makes you look unserious. People who saw the video and this report are laughing at [the wire service].
>
> If this is still in the latest report when we put the page together tomorrow, I will point out in the article how [the wire service] misreported a joke.

Hate can obscure accurate reporting. CNN anchor Don Lemon called a Trump's speech in Phoenix a "total eclipse of the facts." Lemon's misrepresentation was laughed at in social media since he apparently had expressed interest in working for Trump but was not selected.

Evidence: Media accentuate narratives

Media focus their lens to affect stories

News coverage is like looking through the lens of a magnifying glass. While what is at the center of the media lens may seem clear, the relationship of the central image to the surrounding area appears distorted.

The media lens magnifies what is reported, forcing out of context all that surrounds it.

Simple repetition complicates the problem as the same story is persistently spread across 24-hours-a-day broadcasts.

Focusing the lens on just one side of an issue reinforces an opinion. Juxtaposing unrelated items reinforces an opinion. Casting a net too broadly reinforces an opinion. Focusing too narrowly reinforces an opinion.

We emailed the wire service on January 25, 2017:

> Dear [wire service rep] . . .
>
> When [the wire service] writes, "There is no evidence to support Trump's claim." there had better be NO evidence to support his claim.

Take Back Your News

In the case of voter fraud, [the wire service is, quite simply, dead wrong.

[The wire service]:
1) should print a correction, and
2) stop using its repetitive and inaccurate statements about no evidence that it appears to use everywhere to demean whomever reporters do not like.

Certainly [the wire service] can find:
1) the Detroit News statements about more votes than registrations,
2) the papers from Old Dominion and James Mason Universities suggesting there are a significant number of voting irregularities,
3) the indication that California doesn't even look for irregularities, and
4) John Fund's 2009 reporting "The investigators found after an 18-month probe that in 2004 there had been an "illegal organized attempt to influence the outcome of an election in the state of Wisconsin."

[The wire service] has left itself open to embarrassing hit after hit.

As a member of [the wire service] I am reminding you I have been documenting [the wire's] malfeasance for months, if not years and [the wire service] has given me nothing in return that it is actually attempting to do better.

Thank you.

The wire service news rep replied that there was no evidence of widespread irregularities in the 2016 election, suggesting that prior year studies were not relevant to this year's election. We replied:

Dear [Wire service rep]:

Thank you for your reply. If [the wire service] chooses to approach scope and focus more sensibly than it has, you have it within your power to help readers.

Pay attention to **scope** and **focus**. I have repeatedly pointed out [the reporters'] misleading use of "but he provided no evidence" when ample evidence existed outside the **scope** of what she chose to look at and **focus** missed the real issue. Focus not on how many votes were questionable and whether they might have turned the election, but rather how to insure the integrity of each vote:
- Was each citizen authorized to vote allowed to vote?
- Was each of their votes accurately counted?
- Were votes canceled by unauthorized voters?

Evidence of media failure

- Is the integrity of voting systems guaranteed?
- Does a reliable audit trail allow votes to be revalidated when concerns are raised?

It is quite possible, when teased out, that we are all on the same page.

Many national journalists seem tetchy when someone dares point out journalism should be neither adversarial nor absent judgment, but approach each story armed with skills and little baggage.

We do not need a range war in the White House Briefing Room. Please help by recognizing constructive criticism.

Thank you again.

In media fixated on preconceived narratives, what actually transpired easily becomes lost in the views. Other media members often reinforce the media frenzy. Watch any White House press conference to see reinforcement in action — gotcha questions followed by countless permutations of the same question.

On August 15, 2017, we emailed:

Hi, [Wire service rep] . . .
> BC-US--Trump,8th Ld-Writethru
> Defiant Trump insists anew: Blame both sides for violence
> Imported: Today, 9:43 pm

is not an accurate reporting of the Trump presser. Why not?
As others have noted the highlights were:
> 1. Not all the demonstrators were neo-Nazis.
> 2. Where will it end. Will we take down statues of George Washington?
> 3. There was violence on both sides.
> 4. Frankly, you don't know everything.

Report it.
Dammit, report it!
Thank you.
P.S. Then you can step back and report how ill-behaved, unprofessional, and unreliable the national press was. If you dare.

Media maps lose accuracy when details are massaged

The mainstream media fails at its task when good questions are left unasked.

On August 13, 2017, we emailed:
> Subject: Charlottesville questions
> Hi, [wire service rep] . . .

It was fascinating to see [the wire service] so fast off the blocks with the standard race-baiters like Jesse Jackson. Why? Why not report the event and save the unsolicited opinions for later?

I am learning more from serious social media than from [the wire service].

Here are some questions for [the wire service]:

Will [the wire service] be reporting that outside media were encouraged to attend, and how they were invited? Apparently media from Indianapolis, for instance, arrived well in advance of the demonstration.

Will [the wire service] report estimates of the number of attendees on each side? I understand that the "demonstrators" were substantially outnumbered by the "counter-demonstrators.

Did the police funnel the demonstrators through the middle of the counter-demonstrators as some witnesses claim?

Did police stand between demonstrators and counter-demonstrators to keep them peaceful and separated?

What sort of preparatory media did [the wire service] receive prior to the event — as spin in advance? And will AP report it?

What statements seemed prepared in advance in anticipation of delivering a canned media response?

Who was bussed in to the protest, how, how many, and who paid for it?

Who funded the counter-protest?

Did [the wire service] notice what seemed to be a coordinated, rapid response on social media, as if this was an Astroturf event.

How is the DOJ investigating the attack on civil liberties?

Thank you.

Media manipulate context

News offers context. You can't use information unless it is connected to a framework that makes it meaningful.

On July 3, 2017, we emailed the wire service that they had left out useful context.

Hi, [wire service rep] . . .

Sometimes a little context helps inform readers. [the wire service] wrote:

Xi's comments in a phone call with Trump follow Beijing's displeasure over U.S. arms sales to rival Taiwan, U.S. sanctions against a Chinese bank over its dealings with North Korea and, most recently, the sailing of a U.S. destroyer within the territorial seas limit of a Chinese-claimed island in the South China Sea.

Evidence of media failure

We added:
> Xi's comments in a phone call with Trump follow Beijing's displeasure over U.S. arms sales to rival Taiwan, U.S. sanctions against a Chinese bank over its dealings with North Korea and, most recently, the sailing of a U.S. destroyer near an island in the middle of the South China Sea.
> **While China claims the island, so do Vietnam and Taiwan. The passage was one of a series of "freedom of navigation" operations held regularly in the South China Sea and around the world.**

Thank you.

Not telling readers of past precedents leaves them without a framework for recognizing patterns of behavior and deciding whether behavior is unusual and worthy of concern.

> Hi, [Wire service representative] . . .
> [Note: How about this lede: President Donald J. Trump followed the precedents of Presidents Clinton and Obama and asked for resignations . . .
>
> WASHINGTON (AP) — Two days before Attorney General Jeff Sessions ordered dozens of the country's top federal prosecutors to clean out their desks, he gave those political appointees a pep talk during a conference call.
>
> Note: Where is your typical-for-Republicans ". . . but offered no evidence . . ."
>
> On Sunday, some Democrats condemned the demand for resignations in highly partisan comments. Maryland Rep. Elijah Cummings, the top Democrat on the House Oversight Committee, suggested Trump might have fired Bharara to thwart a potential corruption investigation, and believed the move added to a lack of trust of the administration.
>
> I have thought about adding editorial notes to the beginning of some [wire service] articles when you drop the ball.
>
> [Editor's note: The Associated Press failed to include the historical context that President Clinton fired 93, Obama about half that, and Elijah Cummings is the one who made unproven accusations during the Nancy Pelosi walk of the Obamacare bill.]
>
> Why "report" the unfounded accusation at all?
> Thank you.

The wire service replied that it was good they had flagged the comments as "highly partisan" but it would have been better to have said there was no support for the accusation.

Rewritten history erases context. What occurred in the past is often germane to what is news today. It needs to be reported if it would add context. Worse than glossing over what happened is omitting some facts to manufacture fiction.

Take Back Your News

The media will also abuse context, repeating a fixed mantra as if it were context when it is irrelevant. Shallow repetitions push memes. The wire service repeated shallow passages about Michael Flynn and Paul Manafort–Trump/Russia investigations although no evidence has connected Trump with Russia and officials have repeatedly denied any connection.

Any comment about potential Russian collusion in the election campaign still refers to the "Trump/Russia investigation."

On March 14, 2017, we emailed the wire service rep:

> Hi, [wire service representative] . . .
>
> [Wire service's] reporting was shown to be a teensy bit shallow. The [wire service] article on the CBO/Ryancare:
>
>> The office has a four-decade history of even-handedness and is currently headed by an appointee recommended by Price when he was a congressman.
>
> Are its writers too young to remember? Didn't Obama have Gruber work with the CBO to shape the proposal to seem better than it actually was?
>
>> https://www.washingtonpost.com/news/fact-checker/wp/2014/11/14/did-jonathan-gruber-earn-almost-400000-from-the-obama-administration/?utm_term=.f4fc9371f2ef
>
> The model, the Gruber Microsimulation Model, is the coin of the realm, in large part because it is similar to the model used by the Congressional Budget Office. That means administration policy-makers could predict with reasonable certainty how CBO would score legislation. Given that legislation in Washington often falls or rises depending on the CBO score, that made this model a very powerful tool for administration officials.
>
> From Stephen Green at Instapundit and from Reason:
>
>> Congressional Democrats used all sorts of trickery to game the CBO score. Peter Suderman wrote in December, 2009:
>>
>>> After the August recess, scores for the various reform proposals improved markedly. Not only were they cheaper, requiring less total spending, they were judged by the CBO to result in net reductions to the deficit. What happened?
>>>
>>> In large part, the answer is that Democrats became more skilled at manipulating the CBO's scoring process. Indeed, they have become so skilled at getting what they want out of the CBO that the office has taken to including strongly worded warnings that the various bills' real costs may not actually match their estimates.
>>>
>>> In the House, Democrats shifted an expensive, unpaid-for "fix" to doctor's Medicare reimbursement rates over to a separate bill. And in the Senate, they backloaded the spending so that its full effects would not be felt in the 10-year window that CBO scores. In the latest Senate bill, 99 percent of the spending would occur in the last six years of the budget window.

Evidence of media failure

> Nor do the scores count the cost of state level Medicaid expansions—$25 billion in the Senate's bill—or of the private sector mandates it imposes, which, according to Michael Cannon, a health policy analyst at the Cato Institute, could add an additional $1.5 trillion to the total.
>
> The bigger issue is that in budgeting, there are multiple realities available: The various scores put forth by the CBO are based on what might be called "legislative reality" — a fictional world in which there are no changes to current law except the bill under consideration, and new legislation is executed to the letter.
>
> Everybody in Washington knew the numbers were no good, but they were good enough to provide the political cover needed to ram through the legislation. The press, for the most part, played along.
>
> Today, Congressional Republicans seem to have not proactively gamed the CBO, and now are stuck in reaction mode, playing defense against the media and their own budget office.

So is [wire service] going to correct the record for readers about how the CBO was gamed to show Obamacare in a false light?

Thank you.

As the waves of time roll over the surface features of news, salient facts get worn away, particularly when they stand against the popular narrative. It's meme-ification of news.

What can appear to be news often omits the substance of that news.

> House Majority Whip Steve Scalise (R., La.) is relearning how to walk after being shot at a congressional baseball practice earlier this year, House Speaker Paul Ryan (R., Wis.) said...

Kristina Peterson, Wall Street Journal, resorts to passive voice to leave out specifics of who shot Scalise and why.

Media compress past and present to warp context

To presume that what happened in the past is properly measured by standards in use today misunderstands what has gone before. A collapsible telescope that works clearly when opened will distort when the front and back lenses are collapsed. Then and now need to be kept separate to appreciate time and its passage.

After the November election we still had to take the wire service to task for not moving on. On November 15, 2016 we wrote:

> Dear [wire service representative] . . .
>
> 1) Please drop "billionaire" from the [wire service] Trump lexicon. For variety, try "President elect" instead.
>
> 2) Gayness is not a relevant attribute that needs to be attached to articles when considering appointments.

3) Your clauses claiming inexperience do you no credit. You do not provide evidence about what experience matters,

4) Please point to the evidence about Bannon. NPR ran some scurrilous rumors in August, but the anti-Semitic hokum has been adequately countered by Jewish co-workers. [Incidentally, I have gotten pointers to more legitimate news from Breitbart.com than from NPR and been led astray more by CNN than by Breitbart.]

I look forward to seeing your Breitbart evidence.

I see that the post election period will be as difficult for corporate journalists -- a group that includes [the wire service] -- as before the election.

When the wire service replied, citing a years-old custody case, we replied:

Hi, [name] . . .

From the same [wire service] article.

As I understand it, [the wire service] is perfectly okay with quoting as authoritative a categorically denied divorce accusation. Swell. -- Sad, but swell.

Looking elsewhere in the article, [the wire service] is perfectly willing to take a headline written by someone else -- David Horowitz, and adequately defended by the author -- who explains the headline not in terms of hatred, but by Bill Kristol's abandonment of the lone Middle East democracy.

[The wire service] needs better editors.

Your article:

> But other elements of Bannon's tenure are getting more attention. Under his leadership, the site pushed a nationalist, anti-establishment agenda and became one of the leading outlets of the so-called alt-right — a movement often associated with far-right efforts to preserve "white identity," oppose multiculturalism and defend "Western values."
>
> The site specializes in button-pushing, traffic-trolling headlines, including one that called conservative commentator Bill Kristol a "Republican spoiler, renegade Jew." Others asked, "Would you rather your child had feminism or cancer?" and "Birth control makes women unattractive and crazy."
>
> http://www.breitbart.com/big-journalism/2016/05/16/horowitz-no-apologies-for-calling-bill-kristol-renegade-jew/

You may think it seems pretty explicit, but I think you missed an opportunity for informative reporting that would help dampen post-election hysteria.

Regards/Stephen

The media penchant to compress time when exercising its opinion reappeared during rehashing of Trump's first judgments about Charlottesville, was made well before pundits, armed with later released evidence, charged Trump with unbalanced or insensitive comments.

Evidence of media failure

Media preconceived narratives replace news

Internet video streaming has allowed viewers more perspectives on reporting news. Those who have seen White House press conferences since the inauguration of President Trump have been treated to an eye-opening display of how White House reporters push narratives favored by either themselves or their bosses.

On May 3, 2017, we emailed the wire service about an unfortunate penchant for narratives:

Hi, [wire service rep] . . .

This is an article of theatrics, not an article of substance. We trimmed most of it out.

Our readers would have been better served by an accurate representation of what is in and what is out rather than how people care to spin the result.

Anyone who watched the Mulvaney press conference could see the leading questions asked by the press and the statements by Mulvaney designed to redirect attention to what was in the bill. AP would have done well to pay attention.

The word "shutdown" was a case in point. Whether or not it would be a consideration in September is not germane to what was agreed upon, but the press -- including [the wire service] was bound and determined to stick a label of future responsibility on someone. That is silly, and not news.

What [the wire service] could have done is ignore spin about who "won" and described, for instance, what is allowed to be done about stopping attempts to enter the country at the Mexican border. Mulvaney was clear. Who "won" is irrelevant, and a construct of poor reporting.

Also interesting is the break with the one-to-one funding that was the guideline in the Obama administration.

Finally, it was worth mentioning, that this is a continuation of a budget set up by Obama and the previous Congress and that the first real Trump proposal, won't happen until September.

[Wire service rep], this was a feeble attempt to fill space on deadline and an inaccurate representation of what was important.

Thank you.

Wire Service article:
> Government-wide spending bill headed for a House vote
> WASHINGTON — A government-wide spending bill that President Donald Trump seemed to criticize Tuesday morning but now calls "a clear win for the American people" is headed for a House vote.

Take Back Your News

The House is scheduled to vote on the bipartisan $1.1 trillion measure Wednesday afternoon. It is a product of weeks of Capitol Hill negotiations in which top Democrats like House Minority Leader Nancy Pelosi successfully blocked Trump's most controversial proposals, including a down payment on the oft-promised Trump Mexico border wall, cuts to popular domestic programs, and new punishments for so-called sanctuary cities.

The White House instead boasted of $15 billion in emergency funding to jumpstart Trump's promise to rebuild the military and an extra $1.5 billion for border security.

"After years of partisan bickering and gridlock, this bill is a clear win for the American people," Trump said, citing the Pentagon and border money. "This is what winning looks like." Speaker Paul Ryan, R-Wis., also declared victory, but the opinions of top party leaders were not shared by the rank and file.

"From my point of view, we pretty well got our clock cleaned," said Sen. Lindsey Graham, R-S.C.

Earlier Tuesday, however, Trump took to Twitter, angrily reacting to media reports depicting Democrats such as Senate Minority Leader Chuck Schumer of New York as winners in the negotiations. He cited Senate rules that empower minority Democrats and tweeted that the U.S. government "needs a good shutdown" this fall to fix a "mess" in the Senate.

At issue is a mammoth, 1,665-page measure to fund the government through September that largely continues a long-established tradition of bipartisan spending deals that boost funding for medical research, aid for schools, and law enforcement accounts, while defending foreign aid, grants to state and local governments, and the Environmental Protection Agency from cuts sought by tea party Republicans.

Democratic votes will be needed to pass the measure even though Republicans control both the White House and Congress, which made Pelosi and Schumer active and powerful participants in the talks, leading to bipartisan outcomes like a $2 billion disaster aid fund, $407 million to combat Western wildfires, and additional grants for transit projects, $100 million in emergency funding to fight the nation's opioid crisis, and a $2 billion increase for medical research at the National Institutes of Health.

The White House and Sen. Joe Manchin, D-W.Va., both crowed over a hard-fought $1.3 billion provision to preserve health benefits for more than 22,000 retired coal miners and their families, which was included over the opposition of House Speaker Ryan. Pelosi was the driving force behind an effort to give the cash-strapped government of Puerto Rico $295 million to ease its Medicaid burden.

Negotiators on the bill say it looks pretty much like the measure would have looked like if it had been ironed out last year under Obama — save for Trump's add-ons for the Pentagon and the border. Democrats scored some wins as well, and Schumer was quick to run a victory lap in a series of media interviews on Monday that appeared to get under Trump's skin.

"The president is frustrated with the fact that he negotiated in good faith with the Democrats, and they went out to try to spike the football and make him look bad," White House budget director Mick Mulvaney told reporters. Asked about a potential shutdown later in the year, Mulvaney said, "if the Democrats aren't going to behave any better than they have in the last couple of days, it may be inevitable."

Democrats were gleeful at the shutdown talk coming from the highest levels of the White House, which could only increase their leverage in talks on this

Evidence of media failure

summer's round of spending bills for 2018, though Schumer demurred when offered a chance to counter Trump.

"This is a good day, and it's a bipartisan day, so I'm not going to get into finger pointing," Schumer said. "It was a bipartisan negotiation as I said. The leaders — Democrat, Republican, House and Senate — work well together. And why ruin that?"

Their reply said they thought the shutdown business was low in the article and agreed that the "who won, who lost" narrative can be annoying.

Annoying? How about irrelevant?

Media push Agitprop as news

"Agitprop" elides the words "agitate" and "propagandize". The technique has been refined to divide and demoralize a segment of a populace to make it easier politically pass agenda items and even take down governments.

It is a short leap from insinuating information into a news stream to creating events to hijack other events — elbowing aside what might be useful to readers and viewers, replacing content with a different message to drive opinion.

Peter Hasson in the Daily Caller writes:

> Local leaders of Indivisible, one of many "resistance" protest groups formed as a direct response to Trump's election, are organizing thousands of protesters associated with a coalition of left-wing groups ahead of Tuesday's event. In addition to organizing mass protests outside the rally, Indivisible is encouraging protesters to register for tickets for the rally itself, increasing the likelihood that protesters will disrupt Trump's speech, as often happens at Trump's rallies.
>
> Although originally founded by activists not backed by donors, Indivisible's website now states that the group "is a project of the Advocacy Fund," a progressive advocacy group that receives money from the Open Society Policy Center, an arm of Soros' Open Society Foundations. That revelation follows USA Today's reporting in May that leaders of Indivisible and Women's March met with Democracy Alliance, a Soros-led network of left-wing donors, to discuss funding options.[7]

---

[7] http://dailycaller.com/2017/08/22/soros-backed-activists-plan-to-steal-trumps-show-in-phoenix/?utm_campaign=thedcmainpage&utm_source=Facebook&utm_medium=Social

Media fact-starved "fact-checking" isn't news

Sophistry is a bad faith argument.

Politifact wrote that leftists in Charlottesville had a permit to demonstrate. *Politifact* glosses over that the permit was for a different location. They preferred to deem a Trump claim a lie, when actually Trump was correct because demonstrators did not have a permit for the location to which they had migrated.

Politifact used a common news tactic that is to take a statement and debunk it literally in order to deflect from the relevant facts that were true.

Evidence: Media obscure news

Media substitute Information for news

When a secret source provides unverified rumors, it may or may not be news, but it certainly is noise. The media do not keep stats as to how many of their unverified sources have been debunked. They should, every time they resort to one.

Part of the business of reporting news is confirming or debunking conjectures echoed over the Internet. The blogosphere should be used as a media resource. Legitimate questions are often first asked online. The press seldom considers if the questions should be pursued. Ignoring them undermines journalistic trust.

On July 26, 2017 we sent an email:

> Hi, [wire service rep] . . .
>
> Not sure that [the wire service] quite followed through on this article:
>
>> WASHINGTON — Rep. Debbie Wasserman Schultz has fired an information technology staffer following his arrest on a bank fraud charge at a Virginia airport where he was attempting to fly to Pakistan.
>>
>> Wasserman Schultz spokesman David Damron says Irman Awan was fired by the Florida Democrat Tuesday.
>>
>> Awan's attorney, Chris Gowen, confirmed that his client was arrested at Dulles Airport Monday. He says Awan was cleared to travel and had informed the House of his plans to visit his family before the scheduled trip.
>>
>> Gowen says the federal bank fraud count stems from a "modest real estate matter" and is motivated by anti-Muslim bigotry. He's confident Awan "will soon be able to clear his name and get on with his life."
>>
>> An arraignment is scheduled for Aug. 21, according to Gowen.

What is Chris Gowen's association with the Clintons? Apparently, he has done work for the Clinton's before. Are the Clinton's involved here?

Who is handling the case. Is it Steven Wasserman, the brother of Wasserman-Schultz, who is the Assistant US Attorney at the Attorney's office for the District of Columbia? If so, isn't this a conflict of interest? Hasn't he been "investigating" the rest of the Awan family?

And what is the context for the Awans. They have been in the news before, having been the IT guys with access to highly confidential information of Democrats on several committees. That information could have been leaked to media or to others.

Interesting that Awan was kept on by Wasserman Schultz after being fired by so many others.

—

So, is this article shallow on purpose or because [the wire service] didn't want to Google past news?

Looking forward to the next exciting article on the subject. Perhaps you will let me know why [the wire service] wrote it this way and what will be next.

Thank you.

Media use headlines to obscure

Headlines offered by the media often do not capture the most salient point of the articles.

In this case, "Blacks question Trump outreach delivered to white audiences" seemed more accurate written as, "Black groups cheered by Trump outreach."

August 24, 2016, we sent this email to our wire service:

> Your editors may wish to examine the before and after of the horrifically headlined [wire service] story on Trump and black votes:
> **What [the wire service] sent, with our strikeouts:**
> **Headline:** ~~Blacks question Trump outreach delivered to white audiences~~
> AKRON, Ohio (AP) — Black Republicans cheer Donald Trump for a newfound outreach to African-Americans, but say the GOP presidential nominee must ~~take his message beyond arenas filled with white supporters and~~ venture into the inner cities.
> ~~Many rank-and-file black voters, meanwhile, dismiss the overtures as another racially charged pitch from a campaign aimed exclusively at whites, from Trump's emphasis on "law and order" to his withering critiques of President Barack Obama, the nation's first black chief executive. It was Trump in 2011 who fiercely challenged Obama's U.S. birth.~~

Take Back Your News

~~"Any minority who would vote for him is crazy, ought to have their head examined," said Ike Jenkins, an 81-year-old retired business owner in the predominantly black suburb of East Cleveland.~~

~~Foluke Bennett, a 43-year-old from Philadelphia, went further, labeling the GOP standard-bearer's remarks as "racist," pointing, among other things, to his referencing African-Americans as "the blacks."~~

Trump is scheduled on Wednesday to appear in Jackson, Mississippi, an 80 percent African-American city and capital of the state with the nation's highest proportion of black residents. It is unclear whether he will address black voters directly~~; so far, his appeal to them has been delivered before white audiences in mostly white cities~~.

~~Mississippi is overwhelmingly Republican because of whites' loyalties, as opposed to battlegrounds such as Ohio, Pennsylvania and Florida, states Obama won twice and where the largest cities offer at least a theoretical chance for Trump to pursue marginal shifts among significant black populations.~~

~~Trump has already rejected high-profile speaking slots at the NAACP's annual gathering, along with events sponsored by the Urban League and the National Association of Black Journalists.~~

"He's got to take his arguments to the streets," said Brandon Berg, a black pastor who drove Monday from Youngstown, Ohio, to hear Trump at the University of Akron. Berg said he's an outlier: an undecided black Republican. For most African-Americans, Berg said, Trump must "meet them where they are."

~~It's a well-known electoral conundrum: The United States population grows less white with each election cycle, so to defeat Democrat Hillary Clinton, the New York billionaire must attract more non-white voters or run up an advantage with white voters to a level no candidate has reached since Ronald Reagan's 1984 landslide.~~

~~Obama won 93 percent of black voters in 2012 and 95 percent in 2008, according to exit polls. This year, polls suggest Trump could fare even worse than the Republicans who lost to Obama.~~

Trump has confronted his steep path in the last week, asking minorities, "Give Trump a chance!"

In Wisconsin, he declared to minorities: "You live in poverty, your schools are no good, you have no jobs, 58 percent of your youth is unemployed? What the hell do you have to lose?" He argues illegal immigration disproportionately affects economic opportunities of blacks and Hispanics.

~~In Ohio, he insisted without evidence that foreign "war zones" are "safer than living in some of our inner cities." He pledged a Trump administration would "get rid of the crime," allowing minorities to "walk down the street without getting shot."~~

Calvin Tucker, the lone black GOP convention delegate from Pennsylvania, says Trump's arguments resonate with him. "We need a change agent," said Tucker, 64, of Philadelphia. "He's breaking down his overall economic platform and relating it to African-Americans," Tucker added, extolling the GOP's emphasis on entrepreneurial pursuits. . . .

What we ran ~~run~~, after editing:

Headline: Black groups cheered by Trump outreach

AKRON, Ohio — Black Republicans cheer Donald Trump for a newfound outreach to African-Americans, but say the GOP presidential nominee must venture into the inner cities.

Evidence of media failure

Trump is scheduled today to appear in Jackson, Mississippi, an 80 percent African-American city and capital of the state with the nation's highest proportion of black residents. It is unclear whether he will address black voters directly.

"He's got to take his arguments to the streets," said Brandon Berg, a black pastor who drove Monday from Youngstown, Ohio, to hear Trump at the University of Akron. Berg said he's an undecided black Republican. For most African-Americans, Berg said, Trump must "meet them where they are."

Trump has confronted his steep path in the last week, asking minorities, "Give Trump a chance!"

In Wisconsin, he declared to minorities: "You live in poverty, your schools are no good, you have no jobs, 58 percent of your youth is unemployed? What the hell do you have to lose?" He argues illegal immigration disproportionately affects economic opportunities of blacks and Hispanics

Calvin Tucker, the lone black GOP convention delegate from Pennsylvania, says Trump's arguments resonate with him. "We need a change agent," said Tucker, 64, of Philadelphia. "He's breaking down his overall economic platform and relating it to African-Americans," Tucker added, extolling the GOP's emphasis on entrepreneurial pursuits. . . .

Media misidentify content to avoid reporting

A common political habit is to stall, stall, stall until something can be dismissed as yesterday's news. Too often politicians will try to hang on until people become bored. News media should not fall for the gimmick. When it fits their persuasion, they too frequently embrace it.

On June 8, 2017, we emailed the wire service:

Hi, [Wire service rep] . . .

Did [the wire service] cover and/or report on the House Oversight Committee hearing Wednesday where Sen. Chuck Grassley testified, "The [Justice] Department's belated admission that those 64,000 pages were not privileged, puts the gold seal of authenticity on the House's bipartisan vote to hold the attorney general in contempt."

The abuses of "Fast and Furious" are newsworthy, particularly the validation that former Attorney General Eric Holder, were he in office today, might likely be impeached.

[The wire service] did have in the Daybook:

Wednesday, Jun. 07 9:30 AM House Oversight Committee hearing on six years since Operation Fast and Furious - Hearing on 'Fast and Furious, Six Years Later', with testimony from Senate Committee on the Judiciary Chairman Chuck Grassley; Josephine Terry - mother of killed Border Patrol Agent Brian Terry; Terry Family spokesman (and Brian Terry's cousin) Robert Heyer; and Bureau of Alcohol, Tobacco, Firearms and Explosives Phoenix Field Division Special Agent John Dodson * Operation had the goal of catching weapons-trafficking kingpins, but firearms agents lost track of many weapons they were trying to trace to smuggling ringleaders, with some guns ending up at crime scenes in the

U.S. and Mexico. Former Attorney General Eric Holder was previously found in contempt of Congress over his failure to produce documents for a House Committee on Oversight and Government Reform investigation into the operation

But I saw no follow-up.

Thank you.

The wire service replied that the congressional reporting staff felt it was an old case, noting Congress had already sanctioned [Attorney General] Holder five years ago. We replied:

Hi, [wire service rep] . . .

Ah, the "old case" defense. Obama used that a lot with a compliant media.

That's what the stall was designed to accomplish. [The wire service] has been had.

Isn't the release of a 300 page report with conclusions newsworthy?

[The wire service] doesn't have to be there to report on it. I'll wait.

Thank you.

Media engage in willful ignorance

Sometimes the press will avoid "knowing" what they know so they can write it from a preferred perspective. Why miss an opportunity to miss an opportunity.

On July 15, 2017, we emailed:

Hi, [Wire service rep] . . .

On my Facebook page: "When you read breathless [wire service] reports on Donald Trump, Jr., remember that this Forbes article was available to them a month ago."

http://www.forbes.com/sites/paulroderickgregory/2017/06/19/is-russiagate-really-hillarygate/#3ed64b035cf6

Is Russiagate Really Hillarygate? - Forbes

The most under covered story of Russia Gate is the interconnection between the Clinton campaign, an unregistered foreign agent of Russia headquartered in DC (Fusion GPS), and the Christopher Steele Orbis dossier. This connection has raised the question of whether Kremlin prepared the dossier as part of a disinformation campaign to sow chaos in the US political system. If ordered and paid for by Hillary Clinton associates, Russia Gate is turned on its head as collusion between Clinton operatives (not Trump's) and Russian intelligence. Russia Gate becomes Hillary Gate.

Neither the *New York Times*, *Washington Post*, nor CNN has covered this explosive story. Two op-eds have appeared in the *Wall Street Journal* (Holman Jenkins and David Satter). The possible Russian-intelligence origins of the

Evidence of media failure

Steele dossier have been raised only in conservative publications, such as in The Federalist and *National Review*.

The Fusion story has been known since Senator Chuck Grassley (R-Iowa) sent a heavily-footnoted letter to the Justice Department on March 31, 2017 demanding for his Judiciary Committee all relevant documents on Fusion GPS, the company that managed the Steele dossier against then-candidate Donald Trump. Grassley writes to justify his demand for documents that: "The issue is of particular concern to the Committee given that when *Fusion GPS* reportedly was acting as an *unregistered agent of Russian interests*, it appears to have been simultaneously overseeing the creation of the *unsubstantiated dossier of allegations* of a conspiracy between the Trump campaign and the Russians." (Emphasis added.)

Thank you.

Media omit real news

Since reporting is about making choices, media even makes choices about how it chooses to make choices. Media claim to be introspective and self-regulating but seldom is.

In an old joke, a man who bought a donkey confronted the seller demanding his money back because the donkey wouldn't do anything. Reaching for a two-by-four, the seller whacked the donkey upside its head, telling the buyer, "First have to get his attention."

Not that with national media it makes much difference.

On August 2, 2017, we emailed the wire service:

> Subject: You might enjoy this WH press conf. transcript
> Hi, [wire service rep] . . .
>
> > http://donsurber.blogspot.com/2017/08/sanders-is-voice-trump-needs.html?spref=tw
>
> Here is Tuesday's spanking:
>
> > QUESTION: Sarah, according to the Washington Post, the president tried to change the narrative of what went down in [inaudible] meeting with the Russian lawyer. Can you address that story and tell us did the president really try to do that?
> >
> > SANDERS: Look, the statement that Don Jr. issued is true. There's no inaccuracy in the statement. The president weighed in as any father would, based on the limited information that he had.
> >
> > This is all discussion, frankly, of no consequence. There was no follow up. It was disclosed to the proper parties, which is how the New York Times found out about it to begin with.
> >
> > The Democrats want to continue to use this as a P.R. stunt, and are doing everything they can to keep this story alive and in the

papers every single day. The president, the American people, they voted America first, not Russia first. And that's the focus of our administration.

QUESTION: Can you clarify the degree to which the president weighed in?

SANDERS: He didn't -- he certainly didn't dictate. But, you know, he -- like I said, he weighed in, offered a suggestion like any father would do.

QUESTION: I will follow up on that. Was he aware at the time that Don Jr. had had a meeting that was based on the pretext that he would be promised information that was negative about Hillary Clinton when he suggested that the statement only say that the meeting was primarily about Russian adoption policy?

SANDERS: Like I said, the statement that was issued was true and there were no inaccuracies in the statement.

I think what the bigger question is -- everybody wants to try to make this some story about misleading. The only thing I see misleading is a year's worth of stories that have been fueling a false narrative about this Russia collusion and based -- a phony scandal based on anonymous sources.

And I think that is -- if we're going to talk about misleading, that's the only thing misleading I see in this entire process.

You guys are focused on a meeting that Don Jr. had no consequence, when the Democrats actually colluded with a foreign government like Ukraine. The Democrat-linked firm Fusion GPS actually took money from the Russian government while it created the phony dossier that's been the basis for all of the Russia scandal fake news.

And if you want to talk further about a relationship with Russia, look no further than the Clintons. As we've said time and time again, Bill Clinton was paid half a million dollars to give a speech to a Russian bank, and was personally thanked by Putin for it.

Hillary Clinton allowed one-fifth of America's uranium to -- reserve to be sold to a Russian firm whose investors were Clinton Foundation donors. And the Clinton campaign chairman's brother lobbied against sanctions on Russia's largest bank and failed to report it.

If you guys want to talk about having relations, which you seem obsessed with doing, look no further than there.

If you want to talk about somebody who's actually been tough on Russia, look at President Trump. He wants more fracking, more coal, more energy, a stronger military, a stronger defense. Those things aren't good for Russia.

I think the distinctions are very clear and you guys want to create a narrative that just doesn't exist.

Evidence of media failure

Thank you.

Sanders did hit the press upside the head with a verbal two-by-four — to no avail. Looking at White House press gaggle replays hasn't led any of the members to discernable embarrassment.

Media misdirect readers

As gatekeepers of what gets distributed, media controls the narrative. During an August 22, 2017, speech Trump gave in Phoenix, MSNBC lowered the volume of what Trump was saying and substituted their analysis of his remarks.

Some of Trump's remarks that MSNBC suppressed called out media like MSNBC for throttling his message. MSNBC kept from viewers that TRUMP was upset that outlets like MSNBC kept Trump's news from viewers. They proved Trump's point … and didn't seem to care.

> Donald J. TrumpVerified account @realDonaldTrump
> Last night in Phoenix I read the things from my statements on Charlottesville that the Fake News Media didn't cover fairly. People got it!

In another instance, 300 graduates from Yale wrote an open letter to Secretary of the Treasury, Steve Mnuchin, August 18, 2017, demanding he resign.

On August 20, 2017, the wire service ran an article that excerpted from the original letter and Mnuchin's response. The wire service did not link to the original letters. CNBC, to its credit, did give the full text of Mnuchin's response.[8]

Basically, the press represents the letter and the response with no avenue for readers to drill down to primary sources.

Trump bypasses the controllers to go directly to the people. Twitter is Trump's Fireside Chat. He lets citizens judge whom to believe. With gatekeepers alone, readers never have the opportunity to decide for themselves.

As blogger cboldt commented,

---

[8] https://www.cnbc.com/2017/08/19/mnuchin-trump-does-not-equate-neo-nazis-with-peaceful-protesters.html

These writings belong in history books, and today, they should be used as current events discussion material in middle and high schools. Not as an excuse to argue, but rather as studies in style, substance, and accuracy.

Media misdirect with innuendo

Sometimes the media will use words that intimate a preferred view without actually asserting it—a tactic that obscures what news media really should be saying.

On July 14, 2017, we emailed:

> Dear [wire service rep] . . .
>
> [The wire service] apparently chooses not to write in a straightforward manner. [The wire service] prefers to do the "He said" — which could be interpreted as political rhetoric rather than flat out state the facts:
>
> • Opposition research is standard practice.
> • Other political candidates do it.
>
> Neither could [the wire service] admit that the person that visited Trump had visited many other politicians and government officials, both Republican and Democrat, over the past year about the Magnitsky Act, an issue that was completely unconnected with the campaign.
>
> When [the wire service] conflates those two issues, it leads one to suspect [the wire service] did it on purpose.
>
> It appears to be Trump all the time and the other news be damned:
>
> • [The wire service] did not deal with the apparent unusual intervention by Obama's DOJ chief Loretta Lynch how Natalia Veselnitskaya happened to still be in this country.
> • Nor has [the wire service] pointed out the circumstances that allowed Veselnitskaya stay beyond the legal time to remain in the US.
>
> Compare what you wrote today with what we wrote:
> [The wire service] wrote:
>> Headline: Trump: Son's Russia meeting 'standard campaign practice'
>> WASHINGTON — President Donald Trump on Thursday defended his son's meeting with a Russian lawyer, characterizing it as standard campaign practice and maintaining that "nothing happened" as a result of the June 2016 sit-down.
>>
>> The remarks came in Paris during a joint news conference with French President Emmanuel Macron.
>>
>> "I think from a practical standpoint most people would've taken that meeting. It's called opposition research, or even research into your opponent," Trump said.

Evidence of media failure

Trump said "politics is not the nicest business in the world" and that it's standard for candidates to welcome negative information about an opponent. In this case, he added, "nothing happened from the meeting, zero happened from the meeting."

Meanwhile, the Republican chairman of the Senate Judiciary Committee said he would call on Donald Trump Jr. to testify as part of an investigation into Russian meddling in last year's election.

Sen. Chuck Grassley, R-Iowa, said he wants Trump Jr. to testify "pretty soon," perhaps as early as next week. He wouldn't say what he wants to hear from Trump Jr., but said members aren't restricted "from asking anything they want to ask."

The Judiciary Committee is one of several congressional panels investigating Russian meddling in the U.S. election, along with Special Counsel Robert Mueller.

We ran:

Headline: Trump Jr. Russia meeting 'standard campaign practice'

WASHINGTON — In remarks made in Paris during a joint news conference with French President Emmanuel Macron, President Donald Trump on Thursday characterized his son's meeting with a Russian lawyer as standard campaign practice.

News outlets have begun to report the many lobbying meetings the Russian lawyer had had over the previous months with both Republicans and Democrats.

Opposition research is a standard practice undertaken by members of both major political parties.

Trump added, "nothing happened from the meeting."

The Republican chairman of the Senate Judiciary Committee Sen. Chuck Grassley, R-Iowa, said he wants Trump Jr. to testify perhaps as early as next week. He said members aren't restricted "from asking anything they want to ask."

The Judiciary Committee is one of several congressional panels investigating meddling in the U.S. election, along with Special Counsel Robert Mueller.

Our article was more straightforward and accurate.

Certainly [the wire service] does not want to write ambiguously to create innuendo that comes across as poor journalism to editors and readers.

Thank you.

Media warp with selectively reporting

The UK *Daily Telegraph* website persistently declines to identify names, motives, background of alleged perpetrators of what appeared to be terrorism. At the same time they declined to identify a policeman who killed the Cambirls jihadi, they circled a picture of the back of his head, described his background training, his family relationships, and professional relationships. They claimed the policeman, "was not named for security reasons" but then they, irresponsibly, all but identify him.[9]

Media selectively misquote

Lack of attribution allows reporters to inject their own views into interviews and reports without being held accountable for accusations. They will allege "Some people say...." It is a theatric ploy in which the media will allege disputes to put officials on the spot to manufacture conflict where none exists.

When some reporters wish to elevate authority, they label the speaker as an organization. When they choose to diminish it, they name an individual. "Media Matters" says, rather than David Brock. For authority they elevate the speaker to a corporate level or an agency name.

Agencies, organizations, businesses, etc can't speak. People speak, so name them. Their opinion shouldn't matter any more than any other American or group of Americans.

Sometimes, the media will invoke an organization that once might have been a trusted authority. The Southern Poverty Law Center is an organization with roots back in the 1960s. Who are the people behind the SPLC now? What is the organization being used for now? Why should it be used authoritatively and unquestioningly by any news organization? Can its recent claims be verified?

Sometimes even entire quotations are stage-managed. It was too much even for CNN anchor Don Lemon to remain silent as an on-the-scene producer let his CNN photographer rant on as if he were a protester. Lemon called them out on the air for their duplicity.

Editors will sometimes clip substance from quotations to dramatically change the meaning of what is said.

We emailed the wire service on May 2, 2017, when editing misrepresented what was said.

> Hi, [Wire service representative] . . .
>
> If I google "Kim Trump" and "under the right circumstances" I see that most press reports include Trump's full quotation from Bloomberg.

---

[9] http://www.telegraph.co.uk/news/2017/08/20/hero-cop-gunned-terrorists-former-special-forces-soldier/

Evidence of media failure

[The wire service] does not. [It] omits Bloomberg's explicit, "If it's under the, again, under the right circumstances. But I would do that."

By so doing, it absolutely changes the context of the story.

I can't put [the wire service's] action down to inexperience because reporters and editors certainly were familiar with what CNN, USA Today, and others did.

If it was on purpose, by leaving out context and goals, it was misleading, aggressive, and comes across as malicious.

Thank you.

Here is the original article:

BC-AS--China-US-North Korea,1st Ld-Writethru

BEIJING — China urged the United States and North Korea on Tuesday to make contact "as soon as possible" and ease tensions amid rising belligerence from the two sides over the North's nuclear weapons program.

The call for negotiations from China's Foreign Ministry came after President Donald Trump opened the door to a possible future meeting with North Korea's Kim Jong Un.

Trump told Bloomberg News during an interview that he would be honored to meet with Kim at an unspecified future date "if it would be appropriate."

In response, Chinese Foreign Ministry spokesman Geng Shuang said Washington and Pyongyang need to take concrete steps toward peace and avoid further escalating a crisis that has quickly spiraled into a top global security concern.

China has been pushing for the two sides to back down following a string of missile tests by North Korea and a massive live-fire artillery drill last week that was described as its largest ever.

Across the border, South Korea on Tuesday said a U.S.-sponsored missile defense system is now operational — over China's strong objections. U.S. and South Korean troops conducted joint exercises last month along the North's border.

Against that backdrop, Geng said China has taken note of the more diplomatic messages sent by the Trump administration and considers them constructive.

"Both sides should reach a political resolution as soon as possible," Geng said. "The most effective way of attaining an improvement is to seek ways to re-establish dialogue and contact."

What we will run:
Trump would meet Kim 'under right circumstances'

BEIJING — China urged the United States and North Korea on Tuesday to make contact "as soon as possible" and ease tensions amid rising belligerence from the two sides over the North's nuclear weapons program.

Take Back Your News

The call for negotiations from China's Foreign Ministry came after President Donald Trump said he might meet with North Korea's Kim Jong Un "under the right circumstances." Trump told Bloomberg News during an interview that he would meet with Kim at an unspecified future date "if it would be appropriate."

In response, Chinese Foreign Ministry spokesman Geng Shuang said Washington and Pyongyang need to take concrete steps toward peace and avoid further escalating a crisis that has quickly spiraled into a top global security concern.

The administration has made clear that a non-nuclear North Korea is essential to the security of not only the United States but also to China, Japan, South Korea and other regional neighbors.

China has been pushing for resolution following a string of missile tests by North Korea and a massive live-fire artillery drill last week that was described as its largest ever.

[Note: Reverse the last two grafs] Across the border, South Korea on Tuesday said a U.S.-sponsored missile defense system is now operational — over China's strong objections. U.S. and South Korean troops conducted joint exercises last month along the North's border.

Geng said China has taken note of the more diplomatic messages sent by the Trump administration and considers them constructive.

Media will resort to using unnamed sources that usually have an agenda quite different from public interest. They may couch their decision in their interpretation of "public interest" but that is so easy to twist in one's mind.

On July 15, 2017, we emailed:

Hi, [wire service rep] . . .

https://www.rferl.org/a/rinat-akhmetshin-russian-american-lobbyist-who-met-trumps-son/28617101.html

Interesting. How long has the [wire service] known this guy? Your article says that he told you something Friday but does not say how long [the wire service] has been working with him.

How do you know you are not being played? How do you know you haven't been set up?

How big was this "secret" meeting with Trump Jr.? It seems pretty large for collusion doesn't it? Who attended? Who listened in?

Who else — Republican and Democrat — have these people met? On what topics?

What is the alleged crime? Who else was doing similar things?

When did this "Russian collusion" fan fiction start? Who started it?

Now Akhmetshin, a dual Russian-American citizen who has **both denied and bragged about being a former Soviet military intelligence officer,** is at

Evidence of media failure

the center of a growing scandal reaching high into President Donald Trump's White House.

U.S. media reported that he attended a June 9, 2016, meeting with Trump's son, Donald Jr., accompanying a Russian lawyer who was also seeking to undermine the 2012 law.

Akhmetshin did not respond to an e-mail, text messages, or a voice mail from RFE/RL on July 14. **But he told the [wire service]** that the lawyer, Natalya Veselnitskaya, gave Trump associates at the meeting information on what she said were funds being illegally funneled to the Democratic National Committee and suggested the information could help the Trump campaign.

"This could be a good issue to expose how the [Democratic National Committee] is accepting bad money," Akhmetshin was quoted as recalling Veselnitskaya saying.

Considering how much is known by the [wire service], I am as fascinated by how much of it [the wire service] does **not** report as how much it does. And does what is reported get directed from editors or from reporters?

And about your "Analysis", anyone who has followed politics knows Lanny Davis for the spinmeister he is, that you proffer him as simply, "Lanny Davis, who worked as special counsel to President Bill Clinton during his impeachment hearings" is, as Trump would say, "SAD!" We seldom run [wire service] analyses for their absence of news and overwhelming baseless opinion.

You know, I find it interesting that at our local Air Force base, new commanders were rotated in ever three years or so because they wanted a new set of eyes to review structure and operations and assure they were the best they could be. Sometimes people get stuck in old habits.

Thank you.

Media breaking news is often theater

In the 24-hour news cycle, repetition offers no further insight, just an opportunity to push ads people have already seen and ignored.

Media proffer noise as news

Little interferes with a mainstream media narrative. They are capable of embroidering any event to fit a narrative, regardless of the facts they choose to omit or insert.

The wire service added to a news report, "It was not immediately clear why the president decided to comment on Pakistan." That the reporters care not to know is not news and should have been left out as needless noise.

On August 8, 2017, we emailed:

> Subject: Noise, not news
> Hi, [wire service rep] . . .
>
>> Headline: Trump has escaped Washington, but don't call it a vacation
>>
>> BRIDGEWATER, N.J. — President Donald Trump would like to interrupt his vacation to deliver the following message: Don't call this a vacation.
>> The president has decamped from Washington to his private golf club in central New Jersey. But he has repeatedly pushed back on the idea that this is a relaxing August getaway, posting on Twitter over the weekend: "this is not a vacation - meetings and calls!"
>> Trump's staff has labeled the trip a "working vacation." Aides say Trump is meeting with aides and cabinet members to discuss policy and he is expected to go to New York City next week. They have declined to answer repeated questions about whether he is playing golf.
>
> Funny how [the wire service], ... known to bring every extraneous bit under one headline, doesn't see fit to mention that Trump necessarily moved out of the White House because of the massive disruptive renovations going on.
>
> --
>
> You can send a narrative to readers in so many ways. In this case, We know Trump is taking a vacation, so we will compare it to other vacations.
> We at [the wire service] also want you to know that
> 1: Trump is not working as hard as he says he is, and
> 2: What Trump says is not to be trusted.
> I don't recall you running this:
>
>> http://americandigest.org/wp/220-maga-things-trump-work-first-six-months/#more-1869
>
> ———
>
> [The wire service] is doing itself out of its reputation.

Noise often elbows news aside. Sometimes media will report anything and everything, to keep from reporting news. Good questions that should get asked often are not asked. Why? People email and tweet questions to media, only to have them ignored or sidestepped.

On July 13, 2017, we emailed the wire service:

> Hi, [wire service rep] . . .
>
>> [The wire service] seems to be noticeably quiet after the first, second, and third salvo, missing out on the information that

Evidence of media failure

legitimate bloggers have been uncovering. Is this because [the wire service] is "busy" or because [it] doesn't want to have to backtrack its original theme?

Interesting that Loretta Lynch allowed Veselnitskaya to stay in the state. Interesting how many Democrat and Republican politicians she saw that are not included in [the wire service's] dragnet. Interesting how Veselnitskaya rubbed elbows with the Fusion GPS people.

There is a lot that is interesting that still doesn't make the [wire service] cut. It's just a rehash of the same old echo chamber.

[The wire service] should be embarrassed by the Don Jr. spin of your Trump/religious meeting. Really, now. Is nothing sacred?

Of course not. There was considerable substance in the Sarah Sanders press gaggle exposing the MSM fixations that would have been more useful had it been reported.

> https://pjmedia.com/trending/2017/07/12/five-questions-to-ask-about-the-current-trump-kerfuffle/

Question One. Does agreeing to meet with *any* Russian constitute collusion? Does lobbying by a Russian constitute collusion?

Question Two. What criminal statute covers meeting with Russian private citizens? For that matter, what criminal statute covers accepting opposition research about a candidate?

Question Three What is the massive ethical breach involved here? Was it more unethical than these?

Question Four. Does this photograph indicate collusion with the Russians? Is it only collusion when your name is "Trump"?

Based on the thinness of recent Don Jr. articles, [reporter], et al. might find this timeline useful. Ignore the noise. Glean the substance:

From Reddit, but posted from [there] by Clarice Feldman on Facebook:

Reddit Russian timeline: Reddit:Thanks to /u/Thatman5454 for today's Natalia connections.

> Timeline:Jan 2016 - Natalia Veselnitskaya visa expired. Asked by Senator Grassley of Iowa yesterday:
>
> May 4, 2016 - Trump becomes presumptive GOP nominee https://www.washingtonpost.com/.../the-night-donald-trump-b.../...
>
> May 16, 2016 - Democrat oppo research listed Emin Agalarov as a possible route to draw a connection to Vladimir Putin. Their long game has always been to implicate Trump to Russia through the "shady businessman" angle. https://wikileaks.org/dnc-emails/emailid/10436
>
> June 3, 2016 - According to the full email chain Donald Trump Jr released, Emin Agalarov cold contacted DTJ through Rob Goldstone on June 3, 2016 saying Natalia Veselnitskaya had oppo research damaging to Clinton. Email chain: https://twitter.com/DonaldJTrumpJr/status/884789418455953413
>
> June 9, 2016 - DTJ wanted a call instead but took the meeting on June 9, 2016 which turned out to be under false pretenses and he left after 20 minutes. In the meeting Natalia simply spoke about the Magnitsky Act and Russian

adoptions. Same source.June 14, 2016 - Still with no Visa, Natalia Veselnitskaya is seen sitting behind Obama's Russian ambassador Michael McFaul during a Foreign Affairs Committee Meeting. She is sitting in front of Emin Agalarov who set up the meeting with DTJ. Left side towards the end of the video in tan dress. https://www.youtube.com/watch?v=WtpaGJYQxJYConfirmation today by Russian Ambassador Michael McFaul that she was in fact there: https://twitter.com/McFaul/status/885022490686349315Bonus: Here is a picture posted by Natalia inside traitorous war hawk and fake piss gate dossier pusher Senator John McCain's office in December 2015 https://archive.fo/GFjImBonus: Natalia's law firm works with Fusion GPS who created the "Steele Dossier" aka fake Russian Piss Gate against Trump which was given to the FBI by John McCain. https://www.theguardian.com/…/russian-lawyer-who-met-trump-…

- June 14, 2016 - First reports of "Russian hacking" of DNC servers by the Washington Post who has a $600 million contract with the CIA (Deep state unelected government) https://www.washingtonpost.com/…/cf006cb4-316e-11e6-8ff7-7b…Source (liberal) on WP contract with CIA. Their parent company Amazon has the contract and owns the Washington Post: http://www.huffingtonpost.com/…/why-the-washington-posts_b_…
- July 10, 2016 - Bernie Sanders supporter Seth Rich, who worked on the inside of the DNC and was outspoken against voter fraud and Super Delegates is killed without motive. He is suspected by many to have leaked the documents from the inside to Wikileaks instead of an outside hacker (Russia.) https://archive.is/…/bb71ea32102489ed5ee4142afbf1a6f573e420…
- July 22, 2016 - Wikileaks releases documents from the DNC server including emails from John Podesta detailing how the DNC screwed Bernie Sanders in favor of Hillary Clinton: https://twitter.com/wikileaks/status/756501723305414656…
- July 24, 2016 - DNC Director Debbie Wasserman Schultz resigns in light of the cheating in favor of Hillary. She is immediately hired by Hillary's campaign. https://www.nytimes.com/…/debbie-wasserman-schultz-dnc-wiki…
- November 8, 2016 - Donald Trump becomes President. Queue 9 months of Russia coverage.August 9, 2016 - Wikileaks offers $20,000 reward for information leading to Seth Rich's murder: https://twitter.com/wikileaks/status/763041804652539904…^tfw&ref_url=http%3A%2F%2Fwww.theamericanmirror.com%2Fflashback-wikileaks-offered-20000-reward-seth-rich-tips%2F
- August 9, 2016 - Assange hints that Seth Rich is the leaker (not Russia): https://www.youtube.com/watch?v=Kp7FkLBRpKg
- February 23, 2017 - John Podesta joins the Washington Post: https://www.washingtonpost.com/…/john-podesta-joins-the-w…/…
- May 31, 2017 - FBI Director Comey confirms the DNC denied the FBI access to their servers, even though they were reportedly hacked by a foreign government. The DNC instead hired third party company CrowdStrike to investigate. https://www.youtube.com/watch?v=SqIY8KvuoJo

Evidence of media failure

> July 12, 2017 - Full Circle: The original plot in May 2016 to tie Trump to Putin through Agalarov is being pushed by the media today through the 20 minute meeting with Natalia Veselnitskaya about adoptions: https://www.yahoo.com/.../new-details-emerge-moscow-real-esta...
>
> Thank you.

The wire service rep responded that meetings alone would not necessarily prove collusion.

We replied:

> Yes, [wire service rep] . . .
>
> That is why we had to rewrite what [the wire service] wrote on July 12 to be:
>> WASHINGTON — Pundits and politicians continue to comment about Donald J. Trump Jr.'s release to the public of all emails associated with a brief meeting with a Russian attorney during the campaign last year.
>>
>> Trump Jr. has no official position in government, was not required to release any information, and has not been accused of any crime.
>
> and added:
>> The wording of the emails is curious. Soon after the exchange, the Obama government applied to the FISA Court for permission to "wiretap" Trump Towers. Permission was denied but a reduced application was later granted.
>>
>> Such an email request for a meeting with someone from Russia would likely have been detected by NSA and might have been used to engineer FISA permission to snoop. Members of the Obama administration unmasked and widely distributed such politically sensitive information.
>
> Thank you.

Media replace news with noise

Readers need to ask questions:
- Who wanted this article written?
- What do they want me to believe?
- Why do they want me to believe it?

Editors will differ on choices. Reporters can cover ancillary or related stories, but they need to include the basics. In a campaign, that means reporting the high points of what was said. Responsibility and reputation go hand-in-hand. Writing one article is as powerful as censoring another.

By the middle of August, even CBS News was noting substance of the Trump campaign, tweeting:

> Major Garrett Verified account@MajorCBS:
>> Having been listening since August 2016, objectively best drafted & best delivered @realDonaldTrump speech of campaign. Will resonate.

Our wire service feed did not consider the speech significant enough to mention in their top general headlines:

> **[wire service]-Top-General-Headlines**
> Trump campaign shakes up leadership in latest sign of tumult
> [Wire Service] Sources: Manafort tied to undisclosed foreign lobbying
> 10 Things to Know for Today
> Iran acknowledges Russia using its air base to strike Syria
> Staying ahead of the mold, residents salvage what they can
> Monstrous California wildfire drives over 80,000 from homes
> S. Korea: Senior N. Korean diplomat based in London defects
> Explorers find 2nd-oldest confirmed shipwreck in Great Lakes

A search of the most recent 50 wire service political articles revealed no articles on Trump's speech.

Our newspaper was obliged to look up the Trump Wisconsin speech elsewhere on the Internet. Several passages seemed newsworthy. Quoting the transcript:

> When we talk about the insider, who are we talking about? It's the comfortable politicians looking out for their own interests. It's the lobbyists who know how to insert that perfect loophole into every bill. It's the financial industry that knows how to regulate their competition out of existence. The insiders also include the media executives, anchors and journalists in Washington, Los Angeles, and New York City, who are part of the same failed status quo and want nothing to change.
>
> Every day you pick up a newspaper, or turn on the nightly news, and you hear about some self-interest banker or some discredited Washington insider says they oppose our campaign. Or some encrusted old politician says they oppose our campaign. Or some big time lobbyist says they oppose our campaign.
>
> I wear their opposition as a badge of honor. Because it means I am fighting for REAL change, not just partisan change. I am fighting – all of us across the country are fighting – for peaceful regime change in our own country. The media-donor-political complex that's bled this country dry has to be replaced with a new government of, by and for the people.

Trump also said:

> The war on our police must end. It must end now.
> The war on our police is a war on all peaceful citizens who want to be able to work and live and send their kids to school in safety.
> Our job is not to make life more comfortable for the rioter, the looter, the violent disruptor. Our job is to make life more comfortable for the African-American parent who wants their kids to be able to safely walk the streets. Or the senior citizen waiting for a bus. Or the young child walking home from school.
> For every one violent protestor, there are a hundred moms and dads and kids on that same city block who just want to be able to sleep safely at night. My opponent would rather protect the offender than the victim.

Evidence of media failure

Hillary Clinton-backed policies are responsible for the problems in the inner cities today, and a vote for her is a vote for another generation of poverty, high crime, and lost opportunities.

Trump added:

The Democratic Party has failed and betrayed the African-American community. Democratic crime policies, education policies, and economic policies have produced only more crime, more broken homes, and more poverty. ...

The Democratic Party has taken the votes of African-Americans for granted. They've just assumed they'll get your support and done nothing in return for it. It's time to give the Democrats some competition for these votes, and it's time to rebuild the inner cities of America – and to reject the failed leadership of a rigged political system. ...

We reject the bigotry of Hillary Clinton which panders to and talks down to communities of color and sees them only as votes, not as individual human beings worthy of a better future. She doesn't care at all about the hurting people of this country, or the suffering she has caused them.

The African-American community has been taken for granted for decades by the Democratic Party. It's time to break with the failures of the past – I want to offer Americans a new future.

A search of 250 articles found something that we could heavily edit to report substantive content from the speech:

WEST BEND, Wis. — Donald Trump on Tuesday accused rival Hillary Clinton of ~~"bigotry" and~~ being "against the police," claiming that she and other Democrats have "betrayed the African American community" ~~and pandered for votes~~.

"We reject the bigotry of Hillary Clinton, which panders to and talks down to communities of color and sees them only as votes — that's all they care about," the GOP nominee said in remarks delivered not far from Milwaukee — the latest city to be rocked by violence in the wake of a police shooting.

~~Trump, who is lagging behind in the polls, accused Clinton of being on the side of the rioters, declaring: "Our opponent Hillary would rather protect the offender than the victim."~~

"The riots and destruction that have taken place in Milwaukee is an assault on the right of all citizens to live in security and to live in peace," he said.

[Added from the speech transcript:] "The war on our police is a war on all peaceful citizens who want to be able to work and live and send their kids to school in safety," Trump said. "Our job is not to make life more comfortable for the rioter, the looter, the violent disruptor."

[Moved from further down in the article:] Clinton had said Monday that the Milwaukee protests showed that the nation had "urgent work to do to rebuild trust between police and communities" and said "everyone should have respect for the law and be respected by the law."

In an interview on Fox News Channel, Wisconsin Gov. Scott Walker accused Clinton of "inflaming the situation" with her comments.

"I think people understand in that neighborhood and Sherman Park and in Milwaukee, they want law enforcement to step up and protect them," he said, ~~adding that "statements like that" from Clinton and a "lack of leadership" from President Barack Obama "only inflame the situation."~~

Take Back Your News

Milwaukee's Sherman Park neighborhood erupted in chaos Saturday night after a black suspect **waving a gun** [added] was fatally shot by a black Milwaukee police officer. Businesses burned, gunshots rang out and police in riot gear were pelted with rocks and other objects. ~~The violence continued, to a lesser degree, on Sunday night.~~

~~Clinton campaign spokeswoman Jennifer Palmieri responded with a statement early Wednesday accusing Trump of being the bigot instead.~~

~~"With each passing Trump attack, it becomes clearer that his strategy is just to say about Hillary Clinton what's true of himself. When people started saying he was temperamentally unfit, he called Hillary the same. When his ties to the Kremlin came under scrutiny, he absurdly claimed that Hillary was the one who was too close to Putin. Now he's accusing her of bigoted remarks — We think the American people will know which candidate is guilty of the charge," she said.~~

~~"It just absolutely bewilders me when I hear Donald Trump try to talk about national security,"~~ Clinton said, pointing to Vice President Joe Biden's dissection of Trump's foreign policy at a Pennsylvania event Monday. "What (Trump) often says hurts us. It sends the wrong message to friend and foe alike."

~~Turning to the U.S. Olympic team, she said, "Team USA is showing the world what this country stands for."~~

~~On Tuesday, Trump seized on the riots, accusing Clinton of sympathizing with protesters, who have complained of systemic racism and inequality at the hands of police.~~

Trump, ~~who has so far proven deeply unpopular with black voters,~~ made a direct appeal to them Tuesday: "I'm asking for the vote of every African American citizen struggling in our country today who wants a different and much better future." Democrats, he claimed, have pushed policies that exacerbate poverty and crime.

[**Moved from above**:] Trump said in a speech Monday that the country's national security requirements demanded "extreme" vetting of immigrants seeking admission to the United States, pointing to the threat of the Islamic State group and terrorist elements. ~~Trump's remarks, delivered via teleprompter in a rare departure from his usual freewheeling rally remarks, came after~~ Clinton vowed Tuesday to conduct a national security and foreign policy that Americans could be proud of.

~~"The Democratic Party has failed and betrayed the African American community," he said.~~

~~Trump has stoked tensions during his campaign. He has accused Mexico of sending rapists across the border, has feuded with the Muslim-American parents of an Army captain killed in Iraq and has proposed to suspend immigration by Muslims.~~

~~Trump began his visit to the city with a meeting with local law enforcement officers at the Milwaukee County War Memorial Center on Lake Michigan. Among those present were Milwaukee County Sheriff David Clarke, who penned an op-ed Monday blaming liberal Democrats and the media for the unrest that has rocked the city.~~

~~He told Fox News that the shooting in Milwaukee may have occurred because the officer had a gun to his head.~~

~~"Who can have a problem with that?" Trump said. "If it is true, then people shouldn't be rioting."~~

Evidence of media failure

> Trump's campaign also announced Tuesday that it will finally begin airing its first ads of the general election next week in Florida, Ohio, North Carolina and Pennsylvania.
>
> ~~While polls have shown Clinton building a lead following the Philadelphia convention, Democrats are fearful that a depressed voter turnout might diminish support among the minority, young and female voters who powered Obama to two victories.~~
>
> ~~Clinton said at a voter registration event at a Philadelphia high school that she's "not taking anybody anywhere for granted" in the race for the White House, saying the stakes "could not be higher."~~

The wire service not only buried the lede; it left most of the substance out. Then the wire service muffled the content with Clinton campaign spin and throwaway editorial opinions interspersed throughout the article.

So many opportunities for shallow or devious journalism and the media regularly offers examples of each that even school children could point out were they trained to do so.

School children seem directed away from learning to recognize important patterns in order to study other less significant things that actually make them more susceptible to manipulation.

The next section, Book 2, shows how classes have been institutionalized in many states that replace school subjects of pivotal importance.

The example, distilled mostly from New York State, is being pushed in at least 42 states and around the rest of the world. Although in the midst of change, it will be hard to rid curricula of institutional plaque.

Socrates' question is as relevant today as when he was sentenced to death: "Does education belong to government or the individual?"

Book 2: How schools fail journalism

1. Social Studies: To whom does an education belong?

In George Washington's day, doctors leeched patients. It wasn't the best practice, but it was what doctors had been taught to do.

No surprise. Good teachers usually teach what they were taught to teach. Better teachers go beyond that to challenge students to validate for themselves even what their teachers teach.

Education nurtures good questions that exercise inexperienced minds to discover and revalidate useful answers for themselves.[10]

Schooling presumes credentialed experts already have validated what is worthwhile. Schooling presumes to produce cookie-cutter minions that are, by their definition, "good citizens." Schooling produces graduates that are, despite what advocates promise, "college and career *un*ready."

You can't expect graduates unskilled in analytical thinking and cheated of the patterns of history to become competent journalists.

Over scores of years, reflected in an Orwellian "1984" Newspeak, freedom of speech is celebrated for being absent and analytical thinking has become "thinking" rigidly through an approved critical lens.

The "Framework for Social Studies" recently being adopted by many states plays down history, economics, geography, and political theory.[11] In their place, it develops in impressionable youngsters a set of beliefs that engineer social transformation

---

[10] Matthew Arnold: "getting to know, on all the matters which most concern us, the best which has been thought and said in the world; and, through this knowledge, turning a stream of fresh and free thought upon our stock notions and habits."

[11] National Council for the Social Studies (NCSS) College, Career & Civic Life Framework for Social Studies State Standards (C3 Framework)

toward their approved version of "good citizens" aligned with international attempts to unify the world's schooling.

The National Council for the Social Studies designed the new framework. The NCSS failed to ask, "Does an education belong to the individual or to the State?"

NCSS produced and leveraged into effect an unworkable idea that vastly limits student opportunities and could cripple American culture for a long time.

Organizations that fostered Common Core declined to pursue standards for social studies. The NCSS decided to continue on its own.[12] By design, the NCSS exercise seems mind-numbingly pedantic, decorated with Common Core Literacy Guidelines that mask the switch from useful knowledge to beliefs favored by authorities.

Variations of the framework have been approved in at least 42 states. Each state makes modifications. Similar framework levels still reveal verbal misdirection that obscures how useful content has been replaced:

- Key Understandings — labeled "enduring" offer no reason to endure.
- Inquiry Arc — urges students to ask questions they have no foundation to consider, much less ask, confusing key ideas with undefined principles.
- Themes — pass off buzzwords as "unifying" that do not unify.
- Key ideas — confused with understandings, inquiries, and principles.
- Content Specification — misdirects vendors from what matters to what is desired by officials.
- Practices — shift students' focus to research methods leaving little time for history either as events or history as documented prose narrative of events.
- Requirements — subject New York students to an emotional culture war.

The framework that claims to make children "college and career ready" generates fog more likely to produce unanchored semi-

---

[12] The National Governors Association (NGA) and Council of Chief State School Officers (CCSSO)

articulate drones absent multi-disciplined lessons of experience that lead to wisdom.

Underneath it all, the framework teaches to meet official needs, not student needs.

Students needs matter more:
- Students need to master basic principles of society, laws of economics, and development of political theory.
- They need to become astute enough to demand experts explain themselves clearly.

Let's return to examining the past for principles that help students deduce what they can know, how they should act, and how they should interact with others.

The framework is not the answer, nor was the answer what recently has been taught. That is obvious because academics seem not to be alarmed at the attempted hijacking.

What follows explains why returning content to local control is better than imposing the Frameworks. Local districts offer the opportunity to compete in the crucible of competitive ideas for better alternatives.

Sections below dissect the framework to propose a solution:
- To educate or school
- A culture war
- Key understandings represent cultural bias
- Unencumbered with principles
- Irrelevant themes
- Specifications that misdirect
- Practices that obscure history
- The battle for individuals in society
- Centralized transformation is not education

2. Social Studies: To educate or to school?

The complicated attempt to revise how social studies is taught produced unexpected and unacceptable consequences.

To whom does an education belong is the question that caused Athenian authorities to execute Socrates in 399 BC for daring to ask. When schooling belongs to the state, authorities can mold students to maintain their power. When it belongs to individuals, they learn to recognize and defend against self-serving government. The Social Studies Framework (SSF) is the latest salvo in this ongoing war.

Just as magicians distract audiences with illusions, Framework designers distract using Common Core Literacy Standards. Assiduously adhering to Standards, lessons are filled with material that masks how much useful knowledge has been elbowed aside. Furthermore, complexity covers behavioral training methods that reinforce feelings at the expense of reasoning.

Rather than lift students up, the weight of the material keeps students down. Just like Mark Twain's Tom Sawyer enticed his friends to *want* to whitewash Aunt Polly's fence, SSF advocates conned others to want to change the curriculum. They packed a vision of "college and career ready" full of requirements, key ideas, and themes all monitored by evaluations to measure "achievements":

- Parents want college for their children.
- Districts want federal funding, despite the strings.
- Content producers want yearly income.
- Tech vendors want hardware sales.
- Teachers want cookie-cutter lesson plans, organizers, and computerized test marking.
- Elected officials want control.
- Behavioral educationists want culture molded in their image.

Everyone wins but students, cast deep into the fog by "critical thinking" far different from sound analytical skills. Absent foundational knowledge, students are unprepared to mine history for useful patterns. They don't even know such patterns exist.

Too many teachers seem publicly unperturbed about the flaw. Many are more expert in teaching techniques than they are in history, economics, or political theory and much of what they have been required to teach has been peripheral.

Framework designers may not be ideologically driven. They simply may not believe independent individuals can value community. They prefer docile conformity, not individual humanity allowed to mature.

Citizens should expect real education to arm individuals to defend against such impostors who would chew them up for food.

3. Social Studies: A culture war

Social Studies designers believe education belongs to the government.

For instance, the Social Studies Framework set up Grade 8 students to be targets in a culture war. The New York version mandates 72 requirements. All but two push social transformation:
- 44 push Identity Politics, Class Conflict and Culture Wars
- 12 push Business Oppression
- 19 push Internationalism, Anti-War, and Anti-Imperialism
- 4 push Environmental Issues
- 5 push the advantage of Centralized Government

Eighth grade should cover a rich period of the American experience, from the close of the Civil War to the present. Its focus turns out decidedly narrow.

While some Americans across history have been poorly treated by the politics of the day, Framework requirements don't accurately map cultural experience. Dark chapters exist in American history, but they do not represent the entire book.

Mandated curriculum requirements repeatedly demean America.[13] They elbow aside the wonderful things past Americans worked hard to achieve for their children. Students should be proud of American progress and the country's standing compared to the rest of the world. Instead they are left embarrassed.

- 3 of 44 requirements that dwell on Identity Politics describe displacement of people by those with different views.[14] A more useful history would ask how to address inter-cultural conflict issues yet to be resolved, like institutional fraud, government cronyism, property and political rights.[15]

---

[13] Similar requirements in others states follow the College, Career and Civic Life (C3) Framework for Social Studies State Standards guidelines.

[14] For example: "• Students will examine United States and New York State policies toward Native Americans, such as the displacement of Native Americans from traditional lands, creation of reservations, efforts to assimilate Native Americans through the creation of boarding schools, the Dawes Act, and the Indian Reorganization Act and the Native Americans' various responses to these policies."

- 9 requirements foster anti-war internationalism that is another name for political control by those who came to power using any means. It implies peace is the absence of war when peace is the absence of the need for war.[16]

- 12 requirements magnify entrepreneurial oppressiveness implying a need for increased governmental intervention.[17]

Social studies requirements are superficial, political, and self-serving. Yet they are the operational level where content meets students. Rather than educate, when those requirements are collected, repeated, tested, and assessed, they overwhelm useful patterns of experience and principles derived from them.

4. Social Studies: Key understandings go beyond culture

Having shown how a sample Social Studies unit indoctrinates students to feel embarrassed for America's history, those lessons took their lead from Framework levels, including the top "Key Understandings" level explained here.

The Social Studies frameworks (SSF) claim, "Meaningful social studies . . . are structured around enduring understandings . . . ."[18]

It's circular reasoning to argue understandings are considered enduring because they have been popular and popular because they endure. History is littered with popular bad ideas. "Separate but equal" was once popular. Slavery denounced in lessons today might have been considered an enduring understanding in the 1859 social studies frameworks. Imagine teachers required to use then modern pedagogical techniques to drill slavery into yesteryear's inquiring and eager young minds.

---

[15] Comparing westward expansion to the present-day influx of other cultures, consequences of overwhelming cultures by sheer numbers is also worthy of discussion.

[16] For example: "• Students will examine Wilson's Fourteen Points and investigate reasons why the United States Senate refused to support the Treaty of Versailles, focusing on opposition to the League of Nations."

[17] For example: "• Students will explore the growth and effects of child labor and sweatshops." And "• Students will examine state and federal government responses to reform efforts, including the passage of the 17th amendment, child labor and minimum wage laws, antitrust legislation, and food and drug regulations."

[18] http://www.socialstudies.org/ positions/powerful

Popularity only means beliefs are well–known. Popularity offers neither validation nor justification. The Framework's modern packaging of bad ideas won't make them any more significant.

Unexamined popular traditions embedded into frameworks don't offer students paths to determine their origin or why they have value. Platitudes aren't principles. Beliefs aren't principles. Clichés aren't principles. What the frameworks assume to be principles are convenient fictions used to avoid principles. They don't explain why notions matter or justify them with reasoning others could follow and possibly accept as their own.

To earn cachet as principles, ideas with potential grow from wisdom distilled from hard experience. Patterns that appear significant are then projected into hypothetical futures. Some imagined futures would be silly — Utopian models that collapse, unworkable even in dreams. Others show potential. Those that stand up against both the past and future serve as acting principles until fresh experience demonstrates the need to find something better.

Students develop maturity as they revalidate why certain ideas may be principles. As they become confident in their mastery, they can entertain challenges to them, even across cultures. Framework cultural "understandings" can't be expected to transfer across cultural boundaries.[19]

The frameworks fail to establish persuasive connections with other cultures or individuals and vice versa. Students caught in frameworks multi–cultural moral relativism are left unarmed to defend against criticism by other cultures. The frameworks hollowly celebrate multicultural differences even as they wrongly presume cross-cultural experience is uniform and enduring.

Revalidation is the responsibility of every individual. Worthwhile understandings go beyond culture. Each generation is obliged to revalidate the principles previous generations accepted as fundamental in light of more recent experience.

---

[19] The C3 Framework defines culture to be, "a human institution manifested in the learned behavior of people, including their specific belief systems, language(s), social relations, technologies, institutions, organizations, and systems for using and developing resources." C3-framework-for-social-studies.pdf

This is too important a task to be assigned to elite experts. The frameworks offer no path other than habit for a student to deduce their value or revalidate for the current generation their importance. Revalidation is not even a consideration.

Any worthwhile framework would teach the principle behind an enduring understanding. Students would revalidate the principle that validates the understanding. The frameworks should ask, "Why are traditional understandings foundational?"

That they don't ask accentuates that framework designers simply don't know.

5. Social Studies: unencumbered with principles

Having examined how the Social Studies Frameworks represented cultural biases, not principles, consider the consequence of the absence of principles.

For the Social Studies frameworks, democracy is vexing. Democracy is treated as a principle when it is only a process. Democracy doesn't validate a proposition; it is a way to discuss it.

Democracy codifies the humility that what one thinks just might be wrong. It codifies that even the smallest voice might suggest a better way to an audience tuned to hear it.

Yet for the frameworks, they are obliged to resort to platitudes and noise. For them, a democratic principle is one "that should guide the behavior and values of institutions and citizens in a democracy."[20]

They assert as "principles" adherence to the social contract, consent of the governed, limited government, legitimate authority, federalism, separation of powers, equality, freedom, liberty, respect for individual rights, and deliberation. They don't explain why.

The New York framework asserts democratic principles include dignity for all, equality, fairness, and respect for authority and rules. Such assertions are dangerous because, for instance, diversity is popularly encouraged to a degree that suggests groups have privileges beyond what is extended to individuals.

---

[20] National Council for the Social Studies (NCSS) College, Career & Civic Life Framework for Social Studies State Standards (C3 Framework). Page 99.

Frameworks across the states examine the requirements for living in a democracy but leave unexamined why one should want to do so. The College, Career, and Civic Life (C3) framework wants lessons to explain how a democracy relies on people's responsible participation. The National Council for the Social Studies (NCSS) Executive Summary theme, "Civic Ideals and Practices", wants students to learn the "rights and responsibilities of citizens of a democracy."[21]

Authorities have come to promote democracy as if it were a good in itself. More dangerously, political habit has come to treat democracy as if it legitimizes policy. It does not. History is replete with examples the tyranny of the majority. Approval by a majority only signifies that something is popular, not reasonable or justified.

A major theme of education should be to teach students to detect the difference between a real principle and a false bloom. Anything less is schooling, not education. Frameworks ideas blossom from cultural experience making them simply so-called natural law, unable to explain where principles and ideals come from or why they should be held.

The frameworks do not explain how, if American culture arrived at certain principles, those principles resolve when they compete with other principles at home or abroad. The frameworks are blind to the underlying society that holds different cultures together, allowing them to deal across their cultural boundaries.

The Social Studies Frameworks bandy about "Key Idea" and "Compelling Understanding" concepts erroneously labeled principles. Still others are labeled virtues with no other justification than assertion.

The frameworks presume authorities are authorized to determine the common good. They would have students believe experts know principles when they see them, even if ordinary citizens don't.

---

[21] http://www.socialstudies.org/ standards/execsummary.

6. Social Studies: Irrelevant themes

Having recognized that even the concept of democracy is not well presented in the Social Studies Frameworks, consider how Frameworks Themes obscure.

The Social Studies Frameworks themes are supposed to unify but don't.[22] They offer no useful concepts for students to revalidate and call their own. They rehash subjects and popular notions and misdirect attention away from useful lessons of history, economics, and political theory. These apply to one version, the New York flavor, of the Frameworks, but the concepts and criticisms apply across the scores of versions and even the newer revisions:

Theme 1, **Culture** [NYS: 1. Individual Development and Cultural Identity], resigns itself to moral relativism absent a viable path toward peaceful problem resolution and also presumes group identity matters more than individual identity.

Theme 2, **Time, Continuity, and Change** [NYS: 3], presumes the present day to be the end point rather than just another point along a continuum from the past, through the present, to the future. The missed precept makes institutions, values, and beliefs abstract and distant.

Theme 3, **People, Places and Environments** [NYS: 4. Geography, Humans, and the Environment], the frameworks overlook maps as metaphors for necessarily incomplete mental map every individual uses to make decisions. Once understood that "Sometimes you think you are correct, not because you are correct, but simply because you think you are correct", humility and respect for others become the cornerstones of society.

Theme 4, **Individual development and Identity** [NYS: 2. Development, Movement, and Interaction of Cultures], substitutes external socialized behavior when each individual should be the primary theme. Traction comes within the personal perspective to ask: What can one know? How should one behave? How should one interact with others?

---

[22] Ibid.

Theme 5, **Individuals, Groups, and Institutions** [NYS: 5. Development and Transformation of Social Structures] retreats to the inadequate Greek view that cultural groups define individuals and group activities develop good citizenship. That overlooks that when individuals recognize their limits, they have compelling reason to socialize with others.

Theme 6, **Power, Authority, and Governance** makes no distinction between culture and society, which is necessary to overcome moral relativism between cultures. The minimum behavior at the edge where any two individuals or any two cultures meet defines what is required to legitimize governments, understand limits, and recognize abuse.

Theme 7, **Production, Distribution, and Consumption** [NYS: 8. Creation, Expansion, and Interaction of Economic Systems] presumes economics requires a "system". If individuals decide to do what they are good at and swap surpluses to mutual benefit, that is a fact, not a theory and not a "system." Economic effects are in play whatever a government might plan. Structure need not be governmentalized because trade is the result of human action but not human design. The theme ignores unexpected consequences of over-organization, whether regulators have the information to make good regulations, or whether effective redistribution must be governmentally driven.

Theme 8, **Science, Technology, and Society**, ignores that while science and technology may speed interactions and multiply power, they do not change the underlying society itself. The theme juxtaposes process, knowledge, and organization without justification. That science has caused impact over time is obvious and hardly worth a major theme. More significant are recursive feedback loops, relaxation (damping) cycles, and awareness that knowledge of Mother Nature's laws has put such power in the hands of anyone who cares to use it that we are in a race for civilization because isolation is no longer adequate.

Theme 9, **Global Connections**, suggests such connections are different than those between individuals, groups, cities, states, nations, cultures, and civilizations even though behavior at the edge where any two meet is scalable.

Theme 10, **Civic Ideals And Practices**, is unsettling. Releasing millions of political change agents unanchored to society by the lessons of history is not in the best interest of all our culture has accomplished in many hundreds of years of development. In the frameworks, one learns about the rights and responsibilities of citizens in a democracy but, bizarrely, democracy is an unexamined and assumed given. Authors fail to distinguish between statistical inequality, the opportunity for individuals to achieve greater equality, and the attempts of political elites to play off perceptions of inequality to buy power with Other People's Money or to stifle upward mobility through middle class entrepreneurship. They unleash change for the sake of change.

7. Social Studies: Specifications that misdirect

Having shown that content thematically organized was incidental and not relevant to what should be taught, consider next that content, when specified, is not always as it appears.

Implementation texts for teachers and students are the tip of the educational sword. Mostly created by outside vendors, they arrived pre-designed, with expert representations of advanced behavioral pedagogical techniques. Their complexity creates a barrier to entry to competition.

Central bureaucracies dissemble when they posture that content has been left to local authorities. Districts seldom have the time, curricular expertise, or funding to create the classroom material necessary to compete with outside vendors. Requirements are so strict that local districts are left no practical alternative but to accept implementations that express pre-established voice.

The Social Studies Frameworks and outside vendor implementations are like two non-toxic chemicals that, bound together in binary chemical weapons, turn into poison gas. The EngageNY.org website posted vendor-provided sample social studies content for Common Core English Language Arts (ELA) grades 2-12 lessons raise the same concerns as the Social Studies Framework.

The Grade 2 ELA text breaks the non-fiction contract with readers. A non-fiction contract requires a narrative arc to convey a full and accurate representation of facts. Its read-aloud pushes a pasteurized "Democracy Good" Athenian notion that, even simplified for second grade, undermines essential American principles. Half-truths presented as conventional wisdom promote acculturation that trains impressionable students to favor administration prejudices:[23]

- The authors claim Athens favored education while Sparta favored military training — omitting that in Athens girls were not educated while Sparta educated girls to the same level as boys.

- The authors claim Athens invented democracy, while Sparta was a monarchy — omitting that, before Athens created its democracy, Sparta created a balanced constitution incorporating monarchy, aristocracy, and democracy with checks against all three.

- The authors claim Athens favored peace while Sparta favored war — omitting that city-states including Athens respected Sparta because of its concept of justice and willingness to fight to defend it.

- The authors claim Athens favored individualism and Sparta did not — yet in Athens marriages were arranged while Spartans married for love.

- The authors claim Athens was the seat of reason — omitting that demagogues in Athens drove their democracy to collapse, while Spartans, sensitive to democratic flaws refused to participate in the Athenian call to war.

- On the other side, the authors omit that enforced equality of Sparta, where private wealth was banned, left it without the wealth Athens' economic engine generated that allowed creation of naval power strong enough to take on Sparta.

The authors weave partial truths into a preferred narrative. Peace becomes the absence of war rather than the absence of the need for war. Athenians become lovers of peace, arts, and learning and while the Spartan approach valued different lessons the authors considered less positive. Athenians invent democracy while Spartans are not praised for their concern about democracy's potential for overreach.

---

[23] http://www.p12.nysed.gov/ engageny/k-2-curriculum/G2_D5_ Anthology.pdf

Intentional misrepresentation in business commits fraud; in education it commits social change.

In another sample, ELA reading materials for grades 6-12 purport to teach students about "Evidence-based claims." The lessons repeatedly drill students to scan readings for "evidence" of claims, even though such claims are taken out of context and impossible to validate. They encourage students to cite things that are not true without any way of knowing it. They prepare young minds to put blind trust in oratory easily hijacked by demagoguery.

One ELA reading has American tennis player Venus Williams plead for equal prize money for women. The lessons imply something is wrong with America by omitting that equal prize money already had been awarded 32 years earlier to American women and that her criticism was directed at Great Britain.[24]

A 30-year-old reading from Cesar Chavez from 1984 has lessons that drive readers toward a preferred dramatic narrative. The Grade 7 sample reading offers no alternative evidence to assess the assertions Chavez makes, no defense is offered about his accusations, and nothing suggests the problem is contemporary.

Lessons inform students an evidence-based claim, "States a conclusion you have come to... and that you want others to think about." Each "evidence-based" claim is out of context and based upon a single tenuous unsubstantiated opinion that, repeated often enough, easily becomes believed.

Bogus assertions are not fact, but content reinforces feelings about America. One misrepresentation might be happenstance, two a coincidence, but consistent superficiality spread through every year of middle and high school lessons represents either incompetence or a plot.

8. Social Studies: Practices that obscure history

Having examined shortcomings of many levels of the Social Studies Frameworks, examples show the practices they propose actually obscure how to use history.

---

[24] http://engageny.org/resource/ making-evidence-based-claims-unitccss-ela-literacy-grade-8

Learning how to research is quite different from learning to apply history. The New York State K-12 Social Studies Field Guide proposes half a dozen research practices it encourages with time-consuming pedantry. [1][25][26]

The first is "Gathering, Interpreting and Using Evidence." The prefer students to work with primary sources rather than read authoritative historians who across history have identified potentially useful patterns. Sample lessons, while perhaps authentic, proffer material often out of context, slippery, and overwhelming.

The frameworks also encourage "Civic participation."[27]

Participation is inappropriate for a young or immature student easily manipulated.

Unarmed with patterns that history can offer, they easily enable misgovernment that shows little, if any, respect for citizens. It is dangerous for the frameworks to promote democracy without promoting caution because of the ease with which democracy can be hijacked.

History requires vigilance. A pound of hamburger can be cut many ways and still be hamburger. History can be cut many ways and still be history. However, students may find slicing history one way not be as useful as slicing it differently. Students deserve a cut useful for them, not for state educators, do-gooders, and villains who are revisionist at heart.

Leftist social theorist Antonio Gramsci said that war to remake society takes a long march through cultural institutions — like schools that are susceptible to battlefield shaping. For example, the framework considers equality a principle.[28]

The frameworks advocate practices and precepts of questionable value. They suggest one could support equality with a public

---

[25] New York State K–12 Social Studies Field Guide. https://www.engageny.org/resource/new-yorkstate-k-12-social-studies-field-guide.

[26] The frameworks consider Chronological Reasoning and Causation, Comparison and Contextualization, Geographic Reasoning to be social studies practices as well, but examples fail to tease out their variety so they seem used more for show than anything else.

[27] Ibid. NYS Field Guide. Pg 32.

[28] New York State K-8 Framework. Pg. 33. https://www.engageny.org/resource/new-york-state-k-12social-studies-framework (For PDF download).

demonstration, but which equality: equality of opportunity or equality of result? Too often demonstrators want delivered what enforced equality has never delivered—not just 'a' thumb on the scale of justice, but their thumb on the scale of justice because they consider their thumb the only true thumb.

The frameworks invoke history but they don't respect what history has to offer. For instance, the EngageNY ELA Grade 2 sample by CoreKnowledge dismisses mythology. Youngsters learn names of ancient gods, but not their lessons. Frameworks lessons direct teachers to tell students that "people in ancient times often developed religions as they sought explanations for how things came to be or how things happened in nature . . ." as if gods were fanciful fairy tale creations instead of sturdy beliefs by which ancient youngsters lived and died.[29]

Myths were used to transmit life lessons from one generation to another. Youngsters today form beliefs that are different, but no less sturdy and no less mythic than ancient youngsters.

The life lesson of the killing of Medusa, the Gorgon, is more than a mythical magical tale. Medusa, the gorgon, represents history — an underworld creature, with hair of writhing snakes — amorphous, constantly moving, changing shape, ready to strike at the inattentive, and equally deadly to those who fixed their attention directly at her. History has to be respected, filled as it is with writhing, senseless terror, waiting to be repeated.[30]

Perseus slew Medusa, with gifts from gods Athena and Hermes.
- Looking directly at Medusa could kill as easily as rage and despair from looking too closely at the past could poison the reader. Perseus' mirrored shield softly reflected history keeping hope and invention intact to fashion a more solid future.
- History is far away. We don't live there, but Perseus' winged sandals take us there, even though in time it is distant.
- Invisibility offers the opportunity to learn enough about the need to defend ourselves before we are obliged to do so.

---

[29] http://www.p12.nysed.gov/ engageny/k-2-curriculum/G2_D5_ Anthology.pdf. Page 16.

[30] The American Civil War, with both sides fighting well-reasoned positions founded in the Bible, the Constitution, and history, systematically killed off 600,000 civilian and military sons and daughters, each side convinced of their moral right.

- The sword reminds us that the past, the present, and the future require us to find the courage to stand up for ourselves.

The Frameworks selectively misuse history to further social transformation. "Evidentiary" skills and judgment are exercised to hold the past to present-day standards. History and literature are not simply part of cultural heritage. They are how to plumb the past to discover its weaknesses and marshal its strengths.

Medusa teaches us to use history to better one's own future. History should help one discover patterns of practical use either sharpening thinking or helping label practices tried before and found wanting.

9. Social Studies: The battle for individuals in society

Having teased out the shortcomings of the Social Studies Frameworks, consider why such shortcomings exist.

If they had tried, creators of the Social Studies Frameworks could not have developed a program less suited to teach students history, economics, and political theory. But, then, their goal appears to replace individuality in culture with a communitarian view.

Given a choice between regimentation and initiative they chose uniformity. Uniformity begets conformity. Conformity begets enforced equality of result, never successful over the long term.

The frameworks profess "the importance of educating students who are committed to the ideas and values of democracy"[31] but they never offer a rationale why to commit to democracy. Students are not born committed to democracy and the frameworks do not encourage commitment. The frameworks designers don't care because, different than most of us, they see democracy as a tool to mold citizens their way. They quote:

> As Thomas Jefferson, Horace Mann, John Dewey and other great educators understood, public schools do not serve a public so much as create a public. [Cite.] The goal of schooling, therefore, is not merely preparation for citizenship, but citizenship itself; to equip a citizenry with the knowledge, skills, and dispositions needed for active and engaged civic life.[32]

---

[31] http://www.socialstudies.org/ standards/introduction
[32] http://www.socialstudies.org/ positions/revitalizing_civic_learning

They did not choose to educate individuals to decide how to act responsibly. They chose to produce "good citizens" according to their definition of good. As a result, they drill in so much that contains so little worth knowing.

The difference passes by most citizens because the authors redefine words for their benefit, not yours. Words, as author William Gass said, are how we bludgeon people into food.[33]

Frameworks designers don't have to admit their intent. One political theorist called such educationists *comprachicos*—child-buyers: an allusion to those who, for their own ends, manipulate the minds of children.

Educationists embrace John Dewey's model of learning, his "learn by doing" approach that promoted real world experiences, not just reading and drill. Their "critical thinking" distills away the process of analytical thinking. Dogmatic lessons encumbered schools with a restrictive set of blinders.

Social Studies has been an accident in the making since Dewey became infatuated with communal education before it was exposed as a vehicle of the state. Dewey did not coin the title Social Studies, but he certainly believed in social transformation. The frameworks dovetail with international manipulation pursued because principles necessary for society are not as attractive as central control.

What worked in classical education became *passé* because it was accused of favoring those of higher socioeconomic class. To replace it, designers promote group work and cooperative learning rather than nudge students to think for themselves.

They school the clichés of social responsibility and democracy even if strong individual thinking is the more effective way to deduce what society is, what responsibility one has to society, and what validates processes in democracy.

Their oversimplified version of democracy is seeded with an artificial turf of convenient incomplete, politically correct representations.

- For them, placards speak truth, even when they don't.

---

[33] William Gass. Gertrude Stein and the Geography of the Sentence.

- For them, some people are more equal than others.
- For them, ignorance is knowledge.
- For them, what you know is what you feel and feelings trump good sense.

They ply the scientism of select statistics. They invoke the poetry of slogans to feel but not to think. Theirs is the audacity of convictions.

Postmodern and utopian, they gum up minds with viral ideas that know no national borders. They advocate the paternalistic nudge not to understand but to agree. Their hubris is to believe that while people should be free to make their own decisions, "choice architects" like the government can help people make those choices "better."[34] They presume what they believe is better than history. Their error plays out on a grand scale.

Centralized control is the warning they exceeded their charter. They do not value what they cannot understand. Words are weaponry they use to instill a pernicious misunderstanding of the value of society and negate the individual.

Logic cannot dent their convictions, so it falls to us to laugh at them in public. Once exposed, every individual can judge. Such is real democracy.

10. Social Studies: Social transformation is not education

In summary, it is apparent that a ploy to replace social studies with social transformation serves authorities at the expense of individuals.

Legitimate questions have been raised about 1) Common Core, 2) the quality of past teaching, and 3) newly approved social studies revisions.

1) Common Core is a side issue. It is a logical fallacy to presume that either a) education has failed and Common Core is the only way to fix it, or b) that Common Core is worse than the problem and schools should continue what they are currently doing.

---

[34] Sunstein, Cass. Former head of Barack Obama's Office of Management and Budget's Office of Information and Regulatory Affairs.

2) Setting aside Common Core, teachers who do not engage students positively need to be mentored to success or removed from the classroom.
3) While Common Core Literacy Standards help to assure students do not leave the 3rd grade unable to write, read, and inquire, the integration of the guidelines into social studies frameworks obscures social transformation for which no citizen has voted. Pushing transformation, the frameworks fail to teach basic knowledge, skills, and concepts or validate useful understandings that students need to arm themselves to face the world.

Education unequivocally belongs to the individual. The Social Studies frameworks presume education belongs to the state. The task for teachers, school districts, state education authorities, and academia is to recognize the obligation to individual education. It is to recognize the chants for top-down uniform schooling are meant to keep voters from discovering its flaws.

Social studies used to claim to integrate history, economics, politics and culture to show how people have interacted with each other through the years, so the past could be applied to improve current and future interactions. The National Council for the Social Studies dropped that to promote a self-defined version civic competence that parents, if they understood the consequences, would not choose for their children.

Several attempts have been made over the last hundred years to commandeer education along the lines promulgated by national and international organizations with financial and policy interests in removing education from local hands and transforming it to serve their particular interests.[35] They try to supplant history, economics, political theory, and core lessons about social interaction to promote docility and compliance. What is proposed does not help each student develop knowledge and skills to defend against even the teacher.

Socrates' Apology juxtaposed order and discipline next to responsibility and free speech. Those afraid of speech don't trust people. They don't trust anyone but themselves, giving others no reason to trust them.

---

[35] Eubanks. Robin S. Credentialed to Destroy: How and Why Education Became A Weapon. © 2013. Pp. 131-176.

Socrates' question 'Who has the right to educate students?' is really the question 'Who governs?' Authorities call for order, but order is not judgment so it is about who governs.

Plans to commit mental disarmament have reached the point it would be better to discard the centrally approved Social Studies Frameworks version of civics and return to teach what matters to the children to whom the education belongs.

Social Studies: In summary, bring on laughter

The Social Studies Frameworks being implemented in New York schools have substituted behavioral changes that promote social transformation to replace the knowledge and analytical thinking upon which solid education depends.

When such silliness becomes official, and credentials are brandished to defend it, ordinary people can only resort to laughter.

Bring on *Blazing Saddles!* Bring on *The Producers!* Anything but bring on Social Studies. The approved Social Studies Frameworks are so convoluted, obscure, intricate and shallow it is hard to know where first to laugh:

1. Good citizenship is what authorities say it is.
2. College and career ready is a laudable, magical distraction.
3. Culture wars pushed into students is so selective students might disown their own grandparents for daring to believe the American dream.
4. Understandings are key if they reach Billboard's Top Hits chart.
5. Authorities deem when ideas become principles, and they are to be practiced, not understood.
6. Unifying themes are those that produce followers authorities can motivate.
7. Second graders are best fed incomplete feel good concepts while evidence is anything authorities say.
8. What happened in history is not worth studying and economics is what government does.
9. Centralized control is good for the country even when it isn't good for citizens.
10. Schooling that preserves the government is good for the country.

This is an education parents did not long for and one they had no opportunity to reject.

Take Back Your News

It passed because New York State's Education Department (NYSED) pushed Regents to approve a modified Social Studies Frameworks even after the National Council for the Social Studies (NCSS) that pushed the original was told to pack up and go home by the founders of Common Core — the Governors Association and the Council of Chief State School Officers.

It passed in New York because NYSED created a Content Advisory Panel riddled with special interests and friends of the NCSS. It passed because the letters given to the Regents were equally stacked with shills. It passed because it was "for the children" and made them "college and career ready."

- For ordinary people, an expert is someone who explains things so clearly even we can understand.
- For an academic, an expert is someone so credentialed that when they are obscure, no one dares challenge their silliness.

For the sake of our children, laughter is welcome at any local Board of Education meeting where you describe what your children are obliged to learn.

Book 3: Where news fits in society

The Fabric of Society

The fabric of society is woven, one thread at a time, by each individual who learns what matters and why. The discussion about the fabric of society examines lessons often overlooked in today's schooling:

- What can I know?
- How should I behave?
- How should I interact with others?

Individuals who grasp why give testament to their individuality, not to public schooling or social studies classes. Centralized schooling has come to exhibit supreme disinterest in history, principle, or the individual. Such schooling pursues a different agenda of over-simplification cloaked in complex lessons of peripheral value.

History is a teaming sea of experience that cultures can put to the highest or lowest uses. Because history can be compromised, one must carefully extract life lessons to live by.

Today's lack of moral seriousness is a defect that puts us at risk. Lack of moral seriousness occurs when people assume morality can only spring from religion or from shared cultural experience. That kind of morality may work in a closed community, but gains no traction outside a small circle of believers.

The world is engaged, not in a clash of civilizations, and not even a clash of cultures, but with people who lack understanding about society with others. "Others" may be close friends and neighbors, or foreigners far away. When people differ, we must understand how they differ, pursue where to find society together, and be prepared to defend ourselves if necessary.

When individuals are nudged to deduce from their unique personal experience what matters and why, each personally revalidates what is called "character". Character should not be confused with officially approved social behavior.

When you master character, character masters you.

1. Educating Individuals

The points below address how to inoculate students to defend society with principles they revalidate for themselves. We don't have the habit.

Students are eager to learn. Too bad they find little traction in many everyday lessons. It need not be that way. The themes offered fail to guide and motivate them although threads of wisdom run throughout patterns drawn from human experience.

"College and career ready" might seem a driving force for political adults, but students have more interest in dealing with the simple daily problems of living: what can I know, how should I behave, and how should I interact with others.

Philosophy used to deal with those questions, until schooling became the province of government. As noted earlier, Socrates was put to death in 399 BC by a democratic majority in Athens for daring to ask, "Does an education belong to the individual or to the government?" Does the majority get to decide simply because it is the majority? Or should education arm individuals to defend against intellectual assault from any quarter, including government and its scholastic view.

Too many in government decided to hobble students to make them "good citizens" where "good" is defined by elite officials. When not an individual accomplishment, but a social good, molding people to be docile and compliant falls short of education.

"College and career ready" is not enough. Absent proper society, Science, Technology, Engineering, and Math (STEM) leave graduates no secure environment in which to practice. If one wants to drive a car, it is easy to see why STEM is insufficient:
- If you study the history of cars — that in 1885 Karl Benz invented the motorcar or that the economics of cars — that Henry Ford's

division of labor made automobiles affordable even to his workforce, do you know enough to drive?
- If you study physics or chemistry of cars — that rapid oxidation of complex hydrocarbons releases energy against a piston, or study the language, math, or art of cars, do you know enough to drive?
- If you study teaching techniques — that graphic organizers and testing rubrics improve the success of studying cars — or critical thinking — that meta-cognitive strategies increase one's understanding of cars, do you know enough to drive?
- At the end of the day — through layers of educators, administrators, certifications, mandated curricula, standardized testing, whole language learning, classroom directives, contract provisions, political correctness, and lunch menu restrictions, do you know enough to drive?

The car you need to learn to drive is you. Traditional courses like History, Economics, and Political Theory touch on those issues. But the question that gives traction to individuals and society is:

> *Can you recall an instance in your personal past experience when you thought you were correct and later discovered to your regret that you were mistaken?*

Regardless of age, religion, culture, upbringing, or education, that question nudges one to engage in society with others.

Pushing extraneous material, authorities have squeezed out of the curriculum useful patterns of experience. Patterns help recognize when a "social good" is more likely government gone bad, legitimized by victims gulled to become a voting majority. Rather than learn the hazards of democracy, 2nd Graders learn by rote that democracy is good, majority rules, and democracy legitimizes government action. That is too convenient for government. In a time as politicized as ours, neither Leftists nor Rightists should indoctrinate children.

Present day teachers seldom object because colleges taught them how to teach, but not to revalidate what is taught. Weak curricula leave to chance what students need to know to plan their best future. As Dorothy Sayers, the 1930s mystery writer lectured medievalist said to Oxford University academics:

> For we let our young men and women go out unarmed, in a day when armor was never so necessary. By teaching them all to read, we have left them at the mercy of the printed word. By the

invention of the film and the radio, we have made certain that no aversion to reading shall secure them from the incessant battery of words, words, words. They do not know what the words mean; they do not know how to ward them off or blunt their edge or fling them back; they are a prey to words in their emotions instead of being the masters of them in their intellects.[36]

Teaching subjects alone has left us unable to recognize what schooling has become, and certainly unable to resist the darkening trend.

But all is not lost. Students develop character as they deduce behavior that is positive, instructive, and constructive. Practical wisdoms help us sort out where great thinkers made mistakes and to understand why, within the limits of their time, they might have done so. Traction comes from self-interest.

Proper education offers processes kids understand, admire, and wish to emulate in a deeper way.

2. Individuals create society

Economist and moral philosopher Adam Smith said that we enter into society. In practice, when you master why you as an individual need society, it is society that enters into you. Individuals create society out of sheer need. Individuals created journalism to help them, and also created society. Journalism and society extend out from individuals like concentric circles.

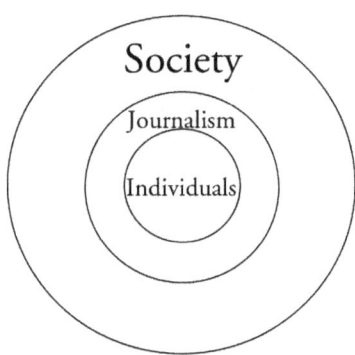

Sometimes those creations contain flaws that mirror the flaws of individuals. Those flaws seem to pass almost unnoticed because

---

[36] Sayers, Dorothy. "Lost Tools of Learning." Web. 17 Jan 2010. <http://www.gbt.org/text/sayers.html>

people are not tuned to see such behavior as flawed. What is worthwhile for an individual is equally important to journalism and society. Skill developed to detect the patterns of bad journalistic habits helps detect similar misbehavior for individuals and society.[37]

The relationship between society and culture is often obscured because society too often is confused with culture. Once people understand how society that underlies culture differs from culture, society's simple elegance becomes clear. Multi-cultural confusion that creates a quagmire of moral relativism muddles society's prospect for a process of peaceful problem resolution.

People who see culture and society the same are like those who see the subject of a photograph in the foreground without sufficient depth of field to see the context background offers.

[38]

Focused on foreground activities alone, they overlook the background represents framework for society. Understanding society generates the courage to defend it against those who, resigned by their actions to living the law of the jungle, would destroy it.

Society is simple. Society is the edge where any two individuals or cultures meet. Society requires no religion, no shared experience, and no natural law.

Individuals need society because each person is alone in one's own consciousness. Even people together are alone. You can't hug

---

[37] Studying journalism exposes "gotcha" techniques, style over sub- stance, ignorance, misuse of statistics, gullibility, historical amnesia, double standards, misrepresentation, misplaced tolerance, misplaced judgment, silence, politics, overused and underused language, rhetorical games, and logical fallacies.
[38] Creative Commons License from: Fir0002/Flagstaffotos

someone close enough not to be alone inside your mind, unsure of what to trust, aided only by pattern recognition skills with which one was born and rationality developed over time.

People are like ships, alien, alone, and adrift on a sea of sense experience, buffeted by the waves.

39

Society can be built projecting forward, in an exercise like linking two ships sailing a storm-tossed sea.

One ship uses a messenger gun to send a thin light line between ships that the second ship uses to return a stronger line. The process is repeated using successively larger lines until the ships are lashed together.[40]

A verbal "messenger line" is simple:

---

[39] Kanagawa. *Great Wave off Hokusai*.
[40] U. S. Navy.

Where news fits in society

Can you recall an instance in your personal past experience when you thought you were correct and later discovered to your regret that you were mistaken?

The question plumbs personal experience to deduce insight into one's process of thinking. Personal experience is not religious dogma, not natural law springing from culture, and not related to the experience of the questioner. An answer invariably leads one to conclude that thinking can be fallible. While not universal, that understanding might as well be. Sometimes you think you are right, not because you are right, but only because you think you are right.

Decisions are not based on reality, but on an abbreviated and incomplete mental map of reality. Self-interest requires one assure one's mental map is as accurate as possible. Self-interest encourages engagement with others who also have come to doubt their own perfection. Society with others can help detect instances where one's thinking may have gone astray. Self-interest encourages community.

That decision-making uses an abbreviated mental map of reality is an idea accessible across all cultural and religious boundaries. It fosters a compelling framework for civilization, a path to honorable decision-making, and creation of virtues. It helps people deduce that long-term interests are served by a character-centered life. Respect is directed inward toward ourselves and toward our treatment of others. Responsibility is directed outward toward friends, school, community, and world.

René Descartes ostensibly said, "I think therefore I am", but he was really saying "I doubt, therefore I am." Doubt and humility are complimentary. One who recognizes doubt becomes humble. Humility comes to those who recognize doubt. Doubt and humility provide compelling incentive to manufacture society with others.

Humility (or doubt) is an understanding that there may be a better way of doing things. Humility represents commitment to the continuous and repeating opportunity for improvement.

Respect (or reciprocity) is an understanding that others can be similarly engaged.

Ingenious creative thinking improves our odds of survival. From simple threads fashioned from humility and a shared sense of need, a sturdy fabric can be fashioned between individuals, independent of their cultures, to encourage a peaceful process of problem resolution. Manufacturing society lifts us slightly above the rest of the animal kingdom and the law of the jungle, to construct a protective umbrella using a process of peaceful problem resolution that others learn to trust and embrace in their self-interest as their own.

Self-interest is why individuals create society. Self-interest motivates learning. Self-interest motivates society with others.

3. Individuals relate to culture through society

Culture and society are different. Cultures form on top of society. Cultures are like the pile of a carpet, varying in color, shape, texture, length, thickness, and material, while society is like the warp and weft threads beneath the pile that hold the carpet together.

Without the warp and weft threads supporting the carpet, all that exists is a pile of pile. Nothing else holds the carpet together.

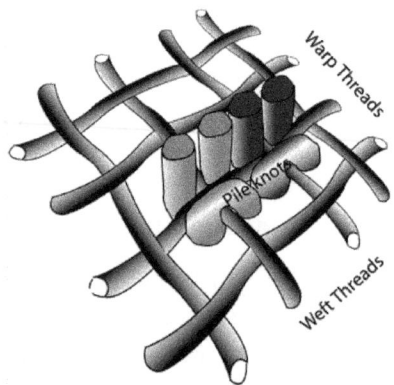

Students validate for themselves that humility and reciprocity are the warp and weft threads. They discover individually why the threads are worth defending. Absent society's supporting threads citizens risk either serfdom or slavery.

Ethical bases are challenged today. Many don't understand why one should be decent. Understanding the minimum requirements for society addresses why one should believe this or why one should do that. When interacting with others who do not share a culture's background and beliefs, culture alone offers no such framework for interaction.

Individuals create ethics. Good reasons for being decent and honorable are deduced from personal experience. There is nothing more to ethics than that individuals matter. Morality springs from the minimum behavior required for society. Morality, or ethical behavior, is derived from:

- **Humility**—The possibility that one just might be wrong, and the humility that falls from that doubt.
- **Reciprocity**—The possibility that society with others similarly engaged can help.

The mechanism is kept honest by conversation with other individuals in society.

Ethical behavior and morality need not be rooted in religion or natural law. The foundations of religion and what cultures call eternal truths operate on top of the framework of society.

Among the things that distinguish humanity from others of the plant and animal kingdom are 1) the skill to communicate complex ideas to each other and 2) the potential to project the consequences of plans for the future. That leads to ethics. Those without such skills revert to the rules that nature requires and nothing more. Be human or be no more than an animal. The choice is individual.

Morality is purely a creation of thought. A seal that snips off the fins of a fish, leaving it a terrified, living, helpless toy to be batted around until boredom and hunger make it lunch, has no conception of good and evil. Good and evil don't exist in the world of seals and fish outside the framework of morality. Life is simply the way things are.

People don't sign up to be moral as if it were a contract. An individual does not so much explicitly subscribe to protection under the moral umbrella as reject it by an explicit anti-social act. An anti-social act as simple as lying or heinous as murder opens oneself to any response in the arsenal of the laws of nature we may choose to use. The perpetrator has chosen the battlefield, not us.

We, in turn, are subject to the laws of nature in our response. We need not reply using the standard of the moral umbrella the offender has rejected, although we may choose to do so. Astute pacifists and generals know war is a nasty place to be and should be avoided, if possible. But those of us who understand morality can defend by any means necessary. And one might survive or both might die. Nature does not care.

Not everyone will be convinced. No compelling reason in the laws of nature or mankind will irrefutably justify morality to any and all men.

One who chooses to act by the laws of lions need not even consent to listen to the arguments in favor of morality. He need not choose to heed anything but that which compels itself to be heard by the laws of nature, if even that.

People cannot be forced to join together under the protection of a moral umbrella. We can only encourage them to understand their long-term security depends upon it.

4. Individuals mature using dynamic processes

The evidence of writing is that humans acquired consciousness over time and not in a single cataclysmic event. Some acquired it, some did not, and, unbelievably, some cultures lost the skill. While there are a lot of things that consciousness is not, psychologist Julian Jaynes holds consciousness to be a very simple thing that includes:

1. The idea of self and the possibility of self-reflection with which we can create a concept of ourselves, and
2. A sense of time for the self we create.[41]

Author Douglas Hofstadter suggests that the emergent phenomena of the brain—those are ideas, hopes, images, analogies, and finally consciousness and free will—are based on a 'strange loop' that we have learned to call recursion: an interaction between the top level reaching back into the bottom level and influencing the thought process for succeeding iterations.[42]

---

[41] Jaynes, Julian. The Origin of Consciousness in the Breakdown of the Bicameral Mind. Boston, MA: Houghton Mifflin Company, 1976. Print.

[42] Hofstadter, Douglas. Gödel, Escher and Bach: An Eternal Golden Braid. New York: Vintage Books, 1980. Print.

M. C. Escher's *Print Gallery*[43] is a visual representation of the recursive process.

Print Gallery shows an individual seen through a gallery window looking at a print of a cityscape that has a person seen through a gallery window looking at a print of a cityscape . . . a description that cycles infinitely in a never-ending feedback loop.

Thinking as we have been talking about it — conscious thought — is acquired. Self-reference is acquired. Narratization — the "I will do this, then I will do that" — is acquired, reinforcing the concept of time, one's place in time, and the concept of recursion. Narratization is what Lucy Calkins teaches successfully in her Columbia Teachers College Writing Workshop, even to students in Kindergarten.

Experience, process, pattern recognition, defensive rhetorical skills, practical experience are all dynamic tools one uses to make more accurate one's mental map of reality the better to make decisions and the better to defend against what is destructive that people, including oneself, might propose.

Metaphors from experience motivate. Useful processes and experience can be mined from what has gone before. In the 1300s, Sociologist Ibn Khaldun, studying historiography, discovered in the flaws of earlier historians the need for humility. He emphasized Hegelian or Marxian dialectic — feedback loops — a process of continuous re-evaluation necessary because — and this is the keystone of wisdom — sometimes we think we are right simply because we think we are right.

Negotiating our way through life, we are interested in the simple daily problems of living such as dealing with people and dealing with the loops that we get into in our own minds. Loops that we have described happen every day in thought. It is positive insight not to blindly trust what we think simply because we are the ones who think a thought.

5. Individuals were haphazardly taught character

Character has been taught ineffectively across history.

---

[43] Escher, M. C. Print Gallery. Lithograph. 1956.

Take Back Your News

In the 1700s, philosopher Immanuel Kant wondered, why it was that moral instruction accomplished so little. Yet, he observed, even little children understand that you should do a thing because it is right.

The challenge is to go beyond rewarding good behavior — which Kant recognized was ineffective — to do something which Socrates called not 'teachable, like geometry,' but teachable in a way, in order to produce not docile sheep but responsible, growing, inquiring citizens.

Fixed rules are incomplete. The Social Studies frameworks consider rules and law to be an enduring understanding. Confucius, 25 centuries ago, knew that approach to be a last refuge.

Confucius determined there were:
1. Natural saints who intuitively knew the way to live.
2. A larger group, to which he considered he belonged, could learn the way.
3. The least capable group remaining required fixed rules of behavior he called laws or ritual.

Current school curricula plays to the last group, supporting order imposed rather than order individually understood and voluntarily applied.

Forcing obedience doesn't teach character. Virtues like 'respect' and 'obedience' sometimes lead to the wrong result. Sometimes 'respect' is not deserved, as when authorities demand action that would be unethical and blind obedience would not be virtuous. 'Obedience' is important, until it comes into conflict with other virtues. If teaching only virtues leads to lack of character, there needs to be a better way.

Teaching vocabulary doesn't teach character. Some suggest courses propose to teach vocabulary to learn to exercise judgment. Teaching the vocabulary of virtue may not develop character by any means other than chance. Learning virtues is different than developing virtue. To teach someone to 'Be this way' or 'Be that way' attempts to teach the result you want to achieve, absent the process to get there. Character isn't promoted through character vocabulists plastering posters in public places:

Loyalty – Using difficult times to demonstrate my commitment to those I serve. That is a platitude that masquerades as wisdom. Who are those served, and why should one commit to them? Commitment became a liability during the Nuremberg trials after World War II.

Wisdom – Making practical applications of truth in daily decisions (versus foolishness). That seems to stretch to find both the vocabulary and the definition.

Integrity – The moral excellence in my life as I consistently do what is right. To decide what is right is left as an exercise to the student.

New "virtues" can be manufactured that are as fact-based as anything virtue vocabulary offers:

Voluptuousness – Using one's beauty to best advantage!

Far from promoting 'Character', virtue-promoters want the warm feeling they get when they convince themselves they promote character. Results don't matter when mastery of the vocabulary of virtues substitutes for character.

Vocabulist virtues are like numbers trying to substitute for mastery of arithmetic. 'Seven! Seven is a good number! Learn seven and arithmetic will certainly follow. Five! Five is another worthwhile number. Master seven, five, and other numbers and arithmetic will magically appear.' Numbers and arithmetic are not the same thing.

Emulation doesn't build character. If to encourage character, one holds up exceptional people to emulate, like Luther Burbank, Martin Luther King, Abraham Lincoln, George Washington, should one emulate their actions or emulate how they decided to act?

How does one decide who to emulate or what trait to emulate? Emulating virtues leads to the appearance of virtue, not to the solid thought processes that lead to why virtuous behavior is worthwhile.

Persistence shouldn't be emulated because Washington had it. Persistence comes from understanding what is important and why. People teach the result they want but not the skills to get there. Teach virtues alone risks overlooking the need to nudge people to recognize for themselves critical processes of thought.

People insist on trying to push character onto others when much of the real work—the work inside their own head — remains unfinished. If you think you know what to do but don't know why, then you don't know character, much less how to convey it to someone else.

A virtue is a shorthand label for the result of thoughtful analysis about a general concept that is, itself, easily acceptable and easily understood from one's own personal experience. Process concepts help people decide what to do so they can plan for their better future.

Virtues result from thinking about yourself, society, life and your place in it. A handful of process concepts allow people to help themselves.

Youngsters may have to be guided by rules until they mature enough to come to see the practical value in it for themselves. They need to develop the skill to consider points of view, and to value thinking as a tool for self-protection.

6. Individuals use experience to produce character

Self–interest leads to a character-centered life. In your own experience you can recall painful experiences that occurred because you thought you were right and later discovered you were mistaken. This is accessible to everyone across cultural and religious boundaries and helps fashion virtues, a compelling framework for civilization, and a path to honorable decision-making.

Point 1: Sometimes we think we are right, not because we are right, but simply because we think we are right. It's possible for you to be wrong, even when you think you are right, because your brain — the tool you use to plan your very best future — decides what to do using not reality itself, but its own internal map of reality. If that map of reality is inaccurate, you can get hurt.

Point 2: Your long-term self-interest depends on maintaining the very best map of reality to work with. Even though other people have different experiences from yours, they can recall their own painful experiences that invariably lead them to the similar conclusions about humility and reciprocity.

Point 3: Those other people live life as acutely as you do. They have the same needs and reason to join together in society. Society becomes mutually beneficial so we can help each other refine our individual mental maps of reality.

Point 4: Reading, writing, and conversation hone skills used to better individual futures. Language is the tool we use to maintain our map of reality, to check it, to refine it, and to represent it on paper so that tomorrow we can look back and see if it makes as much sense then as it does to us today. They capture our expressions of concepts to convey them over immeasurable distance and time to others. Quality of language and language tools matter. The *Trivium* — the first three of the Seven Liberal Arts — refine those tools:

- Grammar is how we express our thoughts clearly.
- Logic is how we check our language for consistency.
- Rhetoric is how we express what we think to others and check what they express to us.

Point 5: A sense of time and one's place in it provides a check on one's map of reality and decision-making.

Point 6: Thinking about thinking recursively is a powerful tool when harnessed constructively.

Point 7: People are responsible for themselves and need to take that responsibility. As children connect language and thought, they are empowered and motivated by practical wisdoms that underlie their conversation:

Dynamic processes are the type of thought that matters. They help prune what does not work and reinforce what does. If drops of water in a river represent that which is understood, then boulders along the shores that guide the flow of knowledge represent the dynamic processes of thought. A handful of practical wisdoms accessible to anybody channel the flow constructively, but we don't habitually teach such things. They include:

1. A sense of self;
2. A sense of time and one's place in it (Represented by the power of narratization);
3. A sense that sometimes one sometimes might be wrong;
4. A sense that other people live their lives as acutely as I do (That the pain another person feels is no different than the pain I feel);
5. A sense that my mental map of reality might be more accurate if I enlist the help of others;

6. A sense that one is responsible for oneself;
7. A sense of the power of recursive thought (That thinking about thinking is a process that can be useful when under control);
8. A sense of the power of tools for thought;
9. A sense that experience can be mined for patterns to help plan;
10. A sense that we are mortal– that just as surely as close as nightfall is we shall be that close to our own deaths;
11. A sense that each person's fundamental purpose is to negotiate his way through life with decent quality of life;
12. That the difference between fantasy and reality is a boundary that must be understood. When you deny what is, you are possessed by what is not.

These are processes kids understand, admire and wish to emulate in a deeper way.

7. How individual character blossoms

One can identify with Michel de Montaigne, inventor of the essay as a literary form in 1585, "If a man remembers how very many times he has been wrong in his judgment, will it not be foolish of him not to mistrust it ever after?"

Montaigne's personal experience is distant from ours, but one can identify a similar pattern in one's personal unique experience. Montaigne said he would run to embrace truth from others when he saw it coming.[44]

He shares a frame of reference despite extreme differences in religion, language, upbringing, culture, time-shift, and almost everything else. People can go beyond the traditions that only carry them so far.

What is perceived as lack of morality is the hollow framework of earlier philosophers crumbling under the heavy weight of more recent criticism like Friedrich Nietzsche's "God is dead" and Jean Paul Sartre's nausea at discovering a universe both Shakespeare and Faulkner called "full of sound and fury, signifying nothing." They found nowhere to turn.

With nothing to replace what had been lost, authorities beat the same drum louder and harder, with no greater expectation of

---

[44] Montaigne, Michel de. Essays. Hammondsworth, Middlesex, England: Penguin Books Ltd., 1958. Print.

success. Brittle rules could be drummed into students, or students could be nudged to develop a process by which they can decide how to respond honorably.

Dynamic process produces citizens better able to recognize the ethics of a situation they find themselves in, and to decide how to respond appropriately to changeable circumstances.

Unique words do not exist to distinguish between culturally dependent traditions called morals, and dynamic process concepts that are paths to moral decisions deduced from humility and reciprocity. If one were to try to find a word to distinguish cultural mores from societal morals, the word "character" fits the morals deduced from humility and reciprocity. Character represents the processes one mind uses to decide how to act toward others. Concepts considered "virtues" map to process concepts:

- Humility, of course, maps to humility, but so does forgiveness.
- Benevolence, compassion, generosity, gentleness, tolerance, justice, loyalty, and others map to reciprocity and a sense that others live their lives as acutely as you live yours.
- Responsibility, truthfulness, sensitivity, dependability, alertness, and sincerity all map to regard for the accuracy of one's mental map of reality.
- Contentment, initiative, joyfulness, patience, map to a sense of time and one's place in it.

Other so-called virtues are skills like rhetoric or worthwhile habits like creativity, orderliness, or endurance. Still other useful understandings are important to know but are not usually classified as virtues:

- Balance, consistency, and simplicity come with perspective.
- Understanding facades and what is possible separate ideas from one's self.
- Recursion and continuous re-evaluation are processes useful for problem solving.

Consider where the courage represented by the Hobbits in Tolkein's *Lord of the Rings* might come from. Characters in books find a well of strength to draw from as surely as they find it in real life.

Thomas Mann's hypothesis in *Magic Mountain* does not have to play out, that our culture creates people that are docile and compliant. Docile and compliant isn't courageous. Joshua Chamberlain at the battle of Gettysburg was courageous, not docile and compliant.

8. Individuals validate character

Civic virtues change over time. If virtues like kindness, wisdom, and integrity do develop character, one has to decide what constructive virtues should be encouraged.

Looking back to Homer, the virtues the poets favored were warlike qualities — legends and fictions that were oracular.

Socrates argued that perhaps one could find a more rational approach. That challenge to the livelihood and power of poets did not sit well, so some, like Aristophanes, misrepresented Socrates as someone who would present the worst case as the best.

Seneca saw justice, moral insight, self-control, and courage as the cardinal virtues in Rome 2000 years ago. In the later Roman republic different actions were at the heart of citizenship that made you a man, or *vir*, in Latin, the root of virtue or *virtus*:

- Piety, because they felt they were a chosen people.
- Honesty, because they could be trusted.
- True, because they kept their word.
- Just, because they believed in equitable application of law.
- Vigilant, because they would fight to protect that which they believed.

Later, in *Sir Gawain and the Green Knight*, Gawain represented the virtuous ideals of the Round Table. The tests of desire and the fear of death faced in Gawain are the same tests that Buddha faced. The medieval pentangle represented five chivalric virtues: fidelity to others, promises, principles, faith, moral righteousness, and personal integrity. Elsewhere they are recorded as generosity, loyalty to and love of others — sometimes called piety, temperance or freedom from lust, courtesy, and benevolence."

Romantics after the Enlightenment, and perhaps of the 1960s wanted to get in touch with feelings as the exercise of virtue. It is possible to overlay in what different cultures consider virtues. Confucian virtues were very similar to those of Socrates in ancient

Greece or Mohandras Gandhi in India — wisdom, justice, moderation, courage.

The question is how to validate that the virtues one would teach are true virtues. Wealth or fame, while popular, are not considered virtues.

Virtues have been described as those traits that cultures value. To discover them, one could go with what has worked and accept what has gone before as gospel.

But which gospel from hundreds of conflicting religions and sects should one accept on faith? The one you believe in, simply because it's yours isn't good enough. George Bernard Shaw sarcastically asked in 1919, in *Heartbreak House*, "Do you think the laws of God will be suspended in favor of England simply because you were born there?"

World War I dashed any vestige of belief that liberal values and technological advancement in natural sciences would lead to steady, civilized society. The world was left in wreckage with cultures in conflict. If one decides to adopt that which other cultures discover to be virtues, one still would have to fashion a virtue detector to test them.

Validation is everyone's task. Reflective judgment is called for, not compliance, to remain continuously open to new information to review that which we have learned regarding what has gone before in light of what over time becomes better understood.

Since politics has become cutthroat competition, people need to develop skills to test its claims. Philosophers say knowing comes from authority, *a priori* understanding, or the contest of science. People need to determine what authority underwrites particular knowledge and value it accordingly.

We may not be able to decide what is 'true' but we can consider what might be 'workable.' To draw on the canvas of the new century, all we have are recollections and patterns recognized from them, massaged by language within its limitations, and used to project consequences of proposed actions into an imagined future.

Philosopher Karl Popper reminded people that science is not about truth, but about doubt. Science is a continuous test for falsity that helps prune ideas that don't stand up to patterns of experience. Otherwise, in one kind of arrogance, people become convinced that their own ambitions are worth the suffering of others. What is true one cannot know, but science helps one understand what is not true.

Phrased another way, society is at risk without the freedom to challenge an idea even though someone may not care to hear. Even so, the freedom to offend does not imply the necessity to do so or determine the form it might take.

When deducing morals, dynamic process concepts encourage thinking about yourself, your place in society, and life itself. A path seeded with process concepts offers practical help that people can easily embrace that ultimately leads to virtuous behavior. Process concepts ignite the spark of self-regulated learning that just this easily pass Socrates' torch on to the next generation.

Journalism is the perfect vehicle to make these essential concepts accessible, and is a division of labor that, for usefully serving individuals and society, would have pleased philosopher Socrates in ancient Greece, sociologist and historian Ibn Khaldun in the Islamic empire, and economist Adam Smith after the modern industrial revolution.

As a surrogate for the individual, journalism fits neatly in a concentric circle between the individual and society.

9. Individual principles matter

A solid foundation of process concepts leads to principles of character among those capable of grasping them. Experience can reveal patterns that, if we choose to recognize and think about them, can give us insight. One needs skills to tell constructive ideas from destructive ones. The skills help produce understanding that inoculates people to defend themselves sensibly.

People often mistake practices for principles. In ancient Athens, the practice of democracy was instituted as a check on consolidated power. Their democracy trusted one–person–one–vote and majority rules, but still fell to tyranny of the majority and votes bought for political advantage.

The real strength of democracy is that it codifies humility as a permanent check to find a better way.

It represents a commitment to freedom of speech because the least of us, given the opportunity, may try to convince others how to improve. Democracy assures the ability to challenge veracity in front of an audience tuned to judge the accuracy of the argument.[45] Brought to consciousness by the charge, individuals choose one side or the other. And, in the end, the penalty for poor reasoning is to have what is said dismissed.

In a democracy, capacity to make individual decisions matters. A representative democracy, when supported by an effective education system, can put forward political candidates with enough character to stand up to a misguided crowd long enough to educate them about what matters. Proper education nudges students to discover what might matter and verify it for personal use. A figurative "friend-or-foe" indicator should warn about those unwilling or unable to value society.

Like democracy, the word freedom is used to stop thinking. Often mistaken as a principle, it is not freedom that we would wish for others, but the opportunity for individuality. Freedom is the result of individuality, not individuality the result of freedom.

Athens in the time of Socrates failed because its democracy, instituted for other reasons, never saw the advantage of institutionalized doubt. Socrates' ancient Greek language didn't have words to make a distinction between culture and society. Plato proposed rules for behavior, but no one could prove their universality. Ancient Rome schooled children with operational skills to become good citizens who spoke well, but Rome still lost its republic.

St. Augustine, after 350 AD, took a different approach suggesting virtues are written on the fleshy tablets of the heart as some kind of natural law, but such laws are culturally dependent and cannot be proven to be absolute.

---

[45] In medieval times, students might argue such things as how many angels could dance on the head of a pin. They didn't care how many angels that might be. They cared to exercise skills used in discussion. The purpose was rhetorical, to exercise detection of logical fallacies. When one was detected, a student would call out, "Distinguo!" to challenge what had been said. Detecting logical fallacies, a core rhetorical skill, is only incidentally part of the ELA frameworks.

Churches have difficulty getting the message across to others beyond their faith because dogma doesn't convince; it compels.

Charlemagne in the 700s developed liberal arts. The *Trivium* nudged students to think using Grammar to put thoughts in order; Logic to see if those thoughts were consistent; and Rhetoric to explain those thoughts clearly to others and analyze their replies. Students then practiced thinking on subjects. The *Trivium* was dropped in the 1500s as it was hoped that by teaching subjects only, students would learn to think.

In the 1300s, Muslim sociologist and historian Ibn Khaldun described government as "an institution which prevents injustice other than such as it commits itself."[46] Embracing a culture's government without reservation is dangerous because it too easily becomes a user of people.

Europeans continued to discount the importance of individuality relative to one's culture as Philosopher Thomas Hobbes in Leviathan (1651) believed the necessary supremacy of government because life in a state of nature was "solitary, poor, nasty, brutish, and short."[47]

Believers in the social compact (social contract) assert that those born into a culture owe their heritage to that culture for the quality of life they enjoy. In 1700s Europe, Voltaire's enlightenment rationality proved insufficient, leading to its overthrow.

Charles Dickens mocked presumptuous "forward-thinking" educators in his 1854 book *Hard Times* that describes attempts to rigidly control education according to the best technical understandings of the day.

Early 20th century educator John Dewey, enamored both with popular democracy and Soviet developments in behavioral schooling, sought to meld the two to develop participatory democracy. His major works were completed before the bloom fell off the communist rose.

---

[46] Ibn Khaldun. *Muqaddimah: An Introduction to History.*
[47] Hobbes. *Leviathan: Or the Matter, Forme & Power of a Com- monwealth, Ecclesiasticall and Civill.*

Teachers after World War II lost confidence in what experience had to teach. They dismissed the advantage the founders brought to the table. They stumbled over the question what should one do if one can't be sure what to trust.

10. Individuals validate governance

Individuals have little reason to trust governors who control schools. Across the better part of a millennium, the institutions of governance challenged to raise human society have instead sown the seeds of their own destruction:

- Politicized religions in the 1500s,
- Absolutism in the 1600s,
- Abstract rationalism in the 1700s,
- Industrialized nation states in the 1800s, or
- Media-manipulated central control in the 1900s

Each refinement of governance failed to clean up the mess left by the previous century, and left a different mess for succeeding centuries to deal with.

The 20th century was an incredible century advancing the sciences — chemistry, physics, biology, psychology, geology, and archeology, engineering, electronics, set and graph theory, gaming, and computation. But socially, we deal with each other much the same as we have for a hundred years: unable to identify how a different culture was destructive or explain why.

Ethics did not mature in the 20th century. Morality never grew beyond Machiavelli and politics became what you can get away with. The '-isms' that come to mind — Libertarianism, Conservatism, Classical Liberalism, or any of the political parties — have not inoculated individuals to defend themselves. Nor have they countered the political class with an alternative that values the individual and explains the tie between individuals and society.

Most unsettling of all, institutional subjects like history, philosophy, art, science, language — the subjects traditionally used to compose alternatives — have themselves become suspect.

You cannot value what you cannot see. If you can't see why individuals need society, manufacturing society will remain unimportant.

It's not hard. It's just not habit. A person keyed to search for a pattern in personal experience is more likely to recognize when that pattern shows a useful way to behave.

A pattern gives you a tool, not a rule. It does not insist how you should behave. Practice to recognize patterns in personal experience is useful with governance, thought, language, ethics, and culture.

People trust their own judgment, when they know it has failed in the past and will likely fail again. Their thinking machinery jumps to conclusions it tries to justify by the flimsiest of means. If one can't trust oneself, how can one trust others equally likely to jump to their own conclusions? Conversely, how can they trust you?

Our country is exceptional because it has confidence in its citizens. Confidence in "We, the people" was and remains the singular most important revelation about the founding of our country.

As a corollary, education is not used to achieve power or to maintain it. Until now. The most powerful advisers in government suggest that manipulation of citizens by government is okay.[48] It is an inversion of the relationship of citizens to their government from which the founders of the country sought to insulate us.

A proper goal for school is not to be "college and career ready". It is not even to create government–approved "good citizens." The goal is to develop maturity and independence that lead one to value and guard society.

The question "Is there room for the individual in society?" was put to bed a century ago, and certainly put away during Ronald Reagan's confrontation with the Soviet Union. After years of dullness and lack of vigilance, the question returned.

People become uncomfortable if the question is recast as "Is society a user of people?" or "Should individuals be suppressed for the advantage of society's powerful?"

Individuals need to claim space in a dominating society. Technology has blinded you; you are connected but not social.

---

[48] Cass Sunstein http://papers.ssrn.com/sol3/papers.cfm?abstract_id=2565892

The Greeks valued liberty and for that liberty were willing to sacrifice everything rather than give up. Too many today would casually trade in liberty for the empty promise of security and the certain slavery of a free lunch, never appreciating its true price.

Ours is a generation so free that it has lost the meaning of freedom, the reason for freedom, and the will to reach for it. As surely as people who have no liberty yearn for it, the people who have liberty handed to them lust for absence of risk.

11. Taking individual responsibility

Humbling, isn't it, to know your consciousness:
- In size fits between the breadth of the universe at 156 billion light years and 10^{16} meters at the level of quarks,
- In time fits between 13.7 billion years of history and an infinite future, and
- In a world is just one of 6,800,000,000 people, many of whom are in need of help.

One's shoulders are not broad enough to carry them all. So, does one give up? How many does one help? Should one help as many as someone else helps? Should everyone tithe?

That could make one feel small, but it puts each individual in charge of that single point in the universe that is the center of their unique consciousness at this one instant in time, gifted with the will to make decisions. Whatever its physics, the center of the universe is here, now, where each unique individual meets it.

Just as you are in charge of your point of consciousness, others are in charge of theirs. It is your responsibility to defend your point and path from others, and, reciprocally, resist the temptation to impose your trajectory on them. You can teach, but you cannot coerce except insofar as others violate the minimums of society. How does one decide what to do?

Socially imposed altruism uses others to pressure individuals into what to do for those in need. Charity is how one decides for oneself what to do. Altruism gives no practical way to answer the question, 'Do you help one, two, ten, or ten thousand?' But if altruism is unworkable, one needs to come to personal terms with generosity to create a reasonable, human alternative that puts one's today, one's life, and that of others in context.

Decide first whether to give up on altruism. Altruism is a premise whose time has never come and never will because others use it too easily as a club to pursue their own interests. One has no obligation to help others — although those who would take advantage of an individual for their own reasons may try convincing them that they do.

Instead, recall Charles Dickens' Ebenezer Scrooge after his epiphany. Scrooge's new perspective on his own existence led to reverence for the situation of others. More alert to one's own journey, one is more sensitive to others, which presents opportunity and personal interest in charity.

Few people read Adam Smith's first book, *Theory on Moral Sentiments* any more, but he recognized that altruism was not an effective virtue. Self-interest brings the truth of experience and, ironically, can be more effective at prompting people to help others. That may sound contrary to observation in today's selfish world, but Smith described a principled position not to be confused with unthinking consumerism. Consider these good people:

- Dr. David Livingstone, the explorer, missionary, and physician of the "Dr. Livingstone, I presume" fame. He worked to abolish the slave trade, educate Africans, and improve their health care.
- Dr. Albert Schweitzer was a theologian, philosopher, musician, physician who organized clinics in west equatorial Africa, and who sought a universal ethical philosophy.
- Mother Theresa ministered to the poor, sick, and terminally ill in Calcutta for almost 50 years.

For whom did Livingstone, Schweitzer, and Mother Theresa do their work? Not the poor as conventional wisdom would have it, but for themselves. Joseph Campbell advised people to follow their bliss. That's what Livingstone, Schweitzer, and Mother Theresa did. They put themselves where they felt they belonged.

Central Africa, India, or our poorest neighborhood may not be where you belong. It is not a role a teacher, a parent, or someone else can press upon you. Not altruism, but your own inquiry into yourself will lead to your particular answer.

Approach the issue obliquely with these questions. Figure how far along a continuum you'd place yourself:

Where news fits in society

- Are you most comfortable when you are busy or idle?
- Are you most comfortable with physical work or mental work?
- Are you most comfortable solitary or social?

Along the X, Y, and Z axes an individual can, respectively, place answers to those questions. There is only one location in the graph that describes one's unique comfort zone for today. It will be different on other days and different for other people. Certainly there are more questions and axes possible, and all of them challenge one to be responsible for setting the mean between the extremes. Aristotle called one's balance point the virtue between the vices. The balance point for each question can change over time. The task is not to put oneself at the center of one continuum or another, but to understand where, along each continuum, is at the time the healthy, comfortable place for one to be.

And if, among the considerations, one finds bliss tending to a garden, tending to family, tending a neighbor, tending to community, or tending to the world, at that moment, that is where one belongs. If it is in the heart of Africa, at a soup kitchen at the Welcome Hall, teaching, writing, or coaching Little League, or simply loving family or friends, go for it! It is not the job of someone else to shame one into altruism. How dare they try!

When you are at peace with your place in the universe, when you are in balance, one will find that Kant's concept of duty is not the powerful motivator. Reciprocity — the sense that others live their lives as acutely as you live yours — is a powerful motivator to help and share, and find great joy in it.

12. Individuals find meaning

A philosopher asked the meaning of life.

To anyone who asks, say, "You selfish, egotistical bastard! You sit there, surveying the world from a very pretty perch, indeed, provided you by everyone who has ever gone before. And you dare to break the gift they have given you. You contemplate abstracts self-indulgently, complain how hard you have it, and that there is nothing to live for, when you cannot see the gift you have been given. You rush to escape, into drugs, alcohol, television, hedonism, small talk, self- pity — anything to stop looping in your head or facing the reality of the meaninglessness of it all. Oh, the horror! Well, grow up! You may not find meaning, but meaning can find you. Your job is to get out of bed, no matter where that bed may be, and say, 'Damn! This is a wonderful day, and I'm going to make the most of it. I am going to laugh, cry, and work myself until I'm happily tired. And, by God, when I die, someone will be able to look back on what I have done, and say thank you for clearing my path just a little more.' "

Uncertainty — that is what we are given. Certainly, we are alone, but we are also together. Sartre reminded us that, although alone, we still have those that we love on whom to practice loving.

Society is so simple, but it is not understood easily or often because appreciating 'why society' takes more steps to independently deduce than it takes steps to see clearly once society's simple elegance is pointed out.

Once you do figure why society matters, you can sell the personal advantage society offers others, and, furthermore, you are armed with the tools and the courage to defend it against those who, resigned to living just the law of the jungle, would destroy it.

To protect society, you need to know what it is and what it does. That arms you to detect and label behavior that would undermine it.

The first weapon of choice is laughter, but every weapon in the arsenal is available to those who would use every weapon in the arsenal against you. Speak softly, but carry a big stick. Keep the big stick but keep it sheathed if possible because you can't predict its unintended consequences. In the end, use the tools you've got.

Whatever authorities may try to impose in schools, we have the tools to independently educate ourselves. Books give you insight, perspective, hope, and companionship. Books nudge you toward a way out. They give you clues to what is wrong. Literature is the way to become sensitive to patterns and the consequences of them. Literature compresses enough experience into a concentrated point that one can manufacture a way to bust out of limitations.

People have every reason to hope. Just as Confucius' carvings on some bamboo could reach out to touch someone 25 centuries later, any insight recorded now can reach out to touch someone else in the unimaginable future.

Where news fits in society

Congratulations! Individuals get to disperse the creeping fog — now that they can survey the past centuries in coffeehouses, work, journalism, art, education, character, individuality, politics, economics, advertising, history, academia, religion, literature, language, community, and culture. Now, make your own hope.

13. Individuals find their place in society

According to today's schooling, your place in society is less as an individual than a participant. To do that, authorities have filtered out of education the best of what has been said and thought. Seldom do students learn to work the complexity of life.

Montaigne, despairs of making sense of himself and speaks to the internal complexity with which every individual must cope,

> "All contradictions may be found in me—bashful, insolent; chaste, lascivious; talkative, taciturn; tough, delicate; clever, stupid; surly, affable; lying, truthful; learned, ignorant; liberal, miserly and prodigal: all this I see in myself to some extent according to how I turn — I have nothing to say about myself absolutely, simply and solidly, without confusion and without mixture, or in one word."

Many ought not trust what they think. Too many people with degrees have not the skill set, attention span, or interest to recognize everyday flaws in themselves, journalism, or society. People like to think they are rational, but fresh evidence arrives every day to question that. Besides, people are not so much rational as learn to use rationality to check their work.

We clutter the curriculum when the central subject worth teaching is how to live.

Discover that you matter. You matter and you need to discover how much you matter. Then you need to learn to defend yourself. Once you discover that you matter, you can shoulder the responsibility to make sure you are up to the task. The resolve not to be taken in by ignorant, selfish game-players depends on you developing process, pattern recognition, defensive rhetorical skills, experience, and a will to work at it.

The tools are simple, yours to discover, and yours to own:
- You plan decisions using a map of reality, not reality itself. That's humbling, because you understand limitations leave the possibility of being wrong.

- You value reciprocity because you recognize others in a similar situation live their lives as acutely as you live yours.
- You have a sense of time and your place in it.
- You value critical judgment.
- You value constructive habits.
- You separate your 'self' from your ideas.
- You disdain facades as unfair to others as others' facades would be unfair to you.
- You value what is possible.
- You value perspective that gives you balance, consistency, and simplicity.
- You value tools like recursion and continuous re-evaluation but recognize their limitations.

Where do you learn to struggle? The myth of Sisyphus tells how the gods condemned him for all eternity to roll a boulder up a mountainside only to have it tumble down again just before it reached the top. The myth is a metaphor — a fiction that tells a truth.

In his interpretation of Sisyphus in *Once and Future Myths*, Phil Cousineau reminds us of something every generation has to learn for itself: It is not what happens to us that matters; what matters is our attitude towards what happens.[49] The story doesn't ennoble suffering, it ennobles struggle.

Struggle is inevitable, and those who learn to see it as an obstacle rather than a burden make life a lot easier for themselves. Cousineau concludes, "the secret of the creative life consists in taking the next step, doing the next thing you have to do, but doing it with all your heart and soul and finding some joy in doing it."

If you forget all the facts and formulas you learn in school, you will nevertheless have grown to be an educated person if you shun the self-absorbed, downward spiral of suffering and develop in yourself, instead, the will to apply yourself each time you approach the mountain.

Minds are not always changed constructively. Sorting out unsound ideas becomes every individual's responsibility.

---

[49] Cousineau, Phil. *Once and Future Myths: The Power of Ancient Stories in Our Lives*. Berkeley, CA: Conari Press, 2001. Print.

Unfortunately, citizens schooled today often are only partially prepared to weigh what others feed them and what they think.

14. Individuals prepare for the future

Individuals today have the advantage of a world of experience that those in the past did not have. That makes it easier to avoid the tar pits others in Philosophy attempted to explore and got caught in. Our predecessors did heavy lifting, but we have incentive others before did not have — the need to act before civil society is trashed.

It is too dangerous to be ignorant about judgment in our age. As powerful weapons become more readily available, this becomes a race between civilization and Armageddon.

Mother Nature doesn't care if we succeed, but we do. We care for ourselves and for our children. Nor can we put off our work, now that isolation no longer protects us. As Jacob Bronowski noted, science has put the power of knowledge in the hands of anyone who cares to learn, so that no longer will a strong box protect our wealth or barred door protect our families.[50]

We are in a race with no guarantee civilization will win. The race is to self-inoculate to recognize and defend against others who would destroy rather than build society; a race to expand civilization with an accessible, compelling message others might decide to value and adopt as their own.

Happily, civilization has a better chance today than ever before, because all it takes is a change of mind. It took only a change of mind for villagers to see that the emperor, parading in what he and his officials supposed was finery, wore no clothes.

Adrift on a communal sea of individual ideas clawing at each other to grow and survive, ideas will be lost, and many should be. The way forward is to sift down to the useful because truth is not so easy to prove. The purpose of logic and rhetoric, the way it used to be taught, is to serve as a sieve to sort out what works from what has not in the past and is unlikely to work in the future.

---

[50] Bronowski, Jacob. *Magic, Science, and Civilization.* New York, NY: Columbia University Press, 1978. Print.

Viral ideas transmit experience that tempers wisdom and culture. The viral nature of ideas is why some pre-computer Balkan states registered typewriters and why the Soviet state later concluded that a country with individual computers could not be restrained.

Individuals motivated by strong ideas can influence people and great nations. The future of humanity depends, not on the success of one country, but on the preservation of sound ideas and sound processes to think about them, until sometime, somewhere, soil is ripe for germination. We touch others with sound ideas. Some Confucian ideas engraved 25 centuries years ago on strips of bamboo projected good sense into the future. That can happen at any time.

Patterns from experience nudge us to embrace the compelling process to engage in life-long learning mastering the tools by which to proceed. Although written about for millennia, they have not always been universally taught.

Confucius taught the sense that other people exist, "Don't do to anybody else what you wouldn't have them do to you" in the form of the Golden Rule phrased as a negative, and much more practical way of expressing the idea. Karl Marx followed Hegel's notion that we must constantly evaluate where we are. He fostered a process by which we can examine the way things are; the way we can use time. Unfortunately, and to the pain of millions, after Marx developed the tool his successors mistook a single iteration, rather than continuous review, to be process.

Across all grade levels and subjects, current courses already contain teachable moments to which practical wisdoms easily attach. Process matters because, as Robert Heilbroner pointed out, when you master logic, logic masters you.[51] It becomes compelling and unavoidable. When you understand that two plus two equals four, nothing will entice you to believe it equals five.

Herodotus believed the Greeks at Thermopylae found courage because they valued liberty so highly that they would rather sacrifice their lives to try to preserve it than live any longer without it. Socrates was a tenacious soldier during the Peloponnesian War

---

[51] Heilbroner, Robert. *Marxism: For and Against*. New York: W. W. Norton & Company, 1980. Print.

because he understood his duty. Defending Little Round Top against all odds at Gettysburg during the Civil War, earned a grammar teacher from Maine, Joshua Chamberlain, the Congressional Medal of Honor.

Courage to defend what is important springs from mastering why something is important. Teachers nudge individuals to master living for themselves and, from that, to discover courage.

A journalism to embrace

Journalism has not failed. Media failed journalism. Editors failed their newspapers and news programs. They insulated you from news and made it difficult for readers and viewers to notice.

Newspapers, many with wire service reports, are read each day by 35 to 40 million people. Almost 30 million viewers watch cable or network television news. Many traditionally accept at face value what is delivered and may not know they should expect better.

The hazard is extraordinary if so many millions of citizens are put at risk because of the quality of news they are fed. Smart people can become petty and careless if the information they are provided is inadequate.

People can pay a heavy price for pettiness. Your future means more to you and your family than to anyone else. If you don't care, who will?

This book offers a framework to see how individuals, journalism and society fit together in elegant simplicity. You can become more cautious. You can defend yourself from "words, words words."

Poor habits may have contributed to the circumstance. Still others would manipulate what people know, incapacitate their ability to think, and render them more docile and compliant.

Reading Book 1 helps prepare you to flush the sewers. As long as pseudo-journalists bury what is said and done, they deserve to be called out for cheating Americans of news. Calling them out stands *for* journalism, not against it. Insist on relevant facts, make connections, and refuse to mimic baseless debate points. Journalism offers much to embrace.

Book 2 encourages you to join those who see how schooling can shortchange students. Graduates should be equipped with adequate tools for thought. Schools degrade when teachers are obliged to teach material that is misleading or irrelevant.

Revisionists propose to remake schools to be "better" through "representational equity" and other rhetorical gimmicks that elbow out useful learning. Their focus on "skills and concepts" reduces what students actually know. Sleepy "mindfulness" does not promote balance and awareness.

Central control of schooling tends to limit the quality of education to what government approves using jaundiced "evidence-based" accountability to guarantee compliance.

Reading Book 3 offers a yardstick to value society with others, cherish it, and protect it. You can see that society depends on individuals, not centralized communitarian rulers.

Donald Trump regularly tweets to get past chaff launched by the mainstream media, Washington apparatchiks, and partisan demagogues. By so doing, Trump — whatever his real or imagined faults — reveals the need to recast American media and politics to reclaim words and meaning.

Too many mistakenly focus on Trump as an anomaly—asking whether Trump happened because people wanted to be clear of Washington balderdash or, as NeverTrumpers might characterize, that Trump the salesman orchestrated a worldview in which he might claim to be the only savior. Such an either/or logical fallacy does not have to be the case.

Hegel's dialectic poses that thesis results in hypothesis, eventually creating synthesis. A cycle of progress requires recognizing shortcomings underlying previous views. The lesson to learn by reviewing what media and wire services have reported is simple: All is lost without individual vigilance.

Examples in this book cover mostly national reporting, but vigilance is called for at every level and elsewhere besides journalism.

People counterfeit journalism because real journalism has value. If it were common practice yesteryear for people to bite a coin to check for a soft tin phony, it is up to individuals to bite each news story to test for authenticity and value.[52]

A journalism to embrace

We met with wire service representatives June 27, 2017, to urge them to grasp that the future of the wire service brand was at risk. Afterwards, we wrote:

Hi, [wire service staff] . . .
Thank you for the opportunity to visit [the wire service] this morning and to discuss both local newspaper and global concerns.
As I reinforced this morning, in the context of the last 500 years, not too many yet recognize our time as pivotal. Nor do they value how journalism fits between individuals and the rest of society.
We editors may wrestle with adjectives, clauses, and structure, but of greater import is how we lay out an accurate "nautical chart" of news for our readers. What a great time to be a journalist. We can feel very proud of what we do.

Freedom must be accompanied by responsibility. Fortunately, individuals can learn to take responsibility for distributed media. They can learn to clear away the rubbish. As that happens, local journalism will survive and flourish.

Journalism reclaimed is a fine gift to give your children and your children's children.

---

[52] Prof. Allen C. Guelzo explained counterfeiters counterfeit currency because real currency has value. He used the analogy to show people counterfeit history because history done well has value. Like currency, people often misuse history on purpose.

Appendices

Appendix 1 — Trump Rome, NY campaign coverage

Covering the Trump speech, the Associated Press—the sole national wire service subscribed to by the Rome (NY) Daily Sentinel—filed a story headlined:

> "Trump amassing delegates who might not be loyal to him"

In the 32 paragraph, 893 word, report, buried in the middle of the report, the sole reference to Trump in Rome was this single sentence:

> "At a rally in Rome, New York, Tuesday evening, Trump angrily denounced Saturday's final allocation of all of Colorado's delegates to Cruz, blasting the party's system as 'rigged' and 'corrupt.'"

The wire service filtered out from its reporting what Trump said to those 5,000 attendees. They chose to report *about* the campaign speech and avoid reporting the content of the speech itself.

Remember, news is a subset of information that presents what you need to know to plan your better future. The wire service didn't report the news. It didn't do its job. When it kept necessary news from readers about what the candidate said, it ceased to practice journalism.

The wire service article continued:

> DES MOINES, Iowa — Already behind the curve in organizing for the Republican convention, Donald Trump has missed crucial deadlines in a number of states to lock up delegates who would stay loyal beyond the first ballot.
>
> Trump's shortcomings in this behind-the-scenes campaign, which hasn't played much of a role in selecting the GOP nominee in decades, could doom his presidential candidacy if he is unable to win the nomination in the initial voting at this summer's national convention in Cleveland.
>
> After that first ballot, most delegates are no longer bound to support the winner of their state's party primary or caucuses — they're free agents who can support the candidate of their choosing.
>
> Most of the actual delegates are elected at state and congressional district conventions run by party insiders, members of the Republican establishment that Trump has run against from the outset of his campaign.

And while Trump's team has had little contact with these loyal party activists, his chief rival for the Republican nomination, Texas Sen. Ted Cruz, has been actively courting them for months.

Trump has spent the past three days hammering at his party's delegate selection process as "unfair."

At a rally in Rome, New York, Tuesday evening, Trump angrily denounced Saturday's final allocation of all of Colorado's delegates to Cruz, blasting the party's system as "rigged" and "corrupt."

Trump's team is only now starting to engage in the delegate selection process, the choosing of the actual people who will attend and vote at the convention. Republicans have already selected delegates in at least nine states. And in others, such as Virginia and Arizona, the deadline to apply to be a delegate has passed.

Indiana's primary, for example, won't take place until next month. But the deadline to become a national convention delegate was in mid-March.

"Are we concerned? Yes, definitely," said Tony Samuel, vice chairman of Trump's Indiana campaign.

The Cruz team feels the opposite.

"Even if (Trump) jumped into high gear, he can't do it," said Shak Hill, a Cruz campaign leader in Virginia. "That's where he's been shut out of the game."

Trump's delegates must vote for him on the first ballot at the convention. But if no one gets a majority, most of the delegates can then bolt if they choose.

Trump is the only candidate with a realistic path to the 1,237 delegates needed to clinch the nomination before the convention. But the path is narrow, and Cruz is working to block him.

Cruz has built an organization of volunteers who are working in state after state to get his supporters selected as delegates, even those who must vote for Trump at first.

Trump is just ramping up his operation, but in some states he's too late.

In Virginia — a state where Trump won the primary — he has missed the deadlines to assemble lists of potential delegates. Cruz, however, has delegate candidates in 10 of Virginia's 11 congressional districts.

The application deadline was last month.

Indiana's primary is May 3, but 27 of the state's 57 delegates — the actual people — have already been selected at congressional district caucuses. The deadline to register as a candidate for delegate was March 15.

In all, at least nine states have picked some or all of their delegates: Colorado, Iowa, Indiana, Kentucky, Louisiana, Michigan, North Dakota, Tennessee and Wisconsin.

Trump has won a total of 100 delegates in primaries and caucuses in these states. In most, however, the candidates had no formal role in selecting the people who will fill those slots.

To help manage the process, Trump's campaign hired a convention manager, Paul Manafort, last week. Manafort helped lead the fight against Ronald Reagan's challenge of then-President Gerald Ford at the 1976 Republican convention in Kansas City.

Manafort has accused Cruz's campaign of strong-arming would-be delegates and said in an interview with Fox News Channel's Sean Hannity airing Tuesday night that he shared concerns with his boss.

"The point that Donald Trump was making is that the process in Colorado was being abused and it's not that the rules themselves were unknown, it's the way the rules were applied," Manafort said, according to a transcript provided

Appendices

by the network. "We're seeing the same mistakes in Colorado, Missouri and Louisiana. And so the mistakes are not really mistakes — it's a pattern."

However, he said Trump was successful in selecting delegates in Michigan, and predicted the same in Nevada.

"In fact, we wiped him out," Manafort said in an NBC interview Sunday. "And we're going to see Ted Cruz get skunked in Nevada."

Former South Carolina Republican Chairman Katon Dawson, who has been publicly neutral in the race, said he's seen no difference in Trump's delegate strategy since Manafort's hire.

Said Dawson, a veteran national GOP strategist, "He's not a household name or miracle worker by any stretch."

Trump won all 50 of South Carolina's delegates. But in order to be a delegate at the national convention, you had to be a delegate at last year's state convention.

"The people that are going to fill those slots were already selected anyway," said Republican political consultant Tony Denny, who has been a delegate to three previous GOP national conventions.

Cruz has already done a lot of groundwork to get supporters selected as delegates in South Carolina.

"The delegate selection process is in their DNA," Denny said of Cruz's ground operation.

To compensate for wire service failure to report the candidate's positions, the *Rome Sentinel* ran an editorial on April 13, 2016:

Headline: Don't sell Donald Trump short

Don't sell Donald Trump short. He brings a different skill set to the campaign for president.

He knows who his opponents are. Speaking to a large crowd at Griffiss Business and Technology Park, he repeatedly took on the national media, Democrats, other Republican contenders, and, forcefully, the Washington establishment.

Trump also knows when to take on his opponents. While he may have laid a few hits on Ted Cruz, his strongest invective was directed at international threats, unworkable government, Democrat cronyism, and the GOP establishment. He made clear that once the nomination is his, Republicans will unite, and once the election is over, citizens will unite against those who economically, politically and militarily might want to take us down.

In advance of Trump's appearance, his campaign cannily disarmed potential protesters who might be abetted by national news looking for headlines. Trump's spokesman said they believe in free speech, but that this was a private event paid for by Trump. He advised attendees not to touch or harm protesters but to outshout them until Secret Service, police, and sheriff officers could escort them out.

Trump hit hard in repetitive Twitter length phrases:

"Nobody is voting for a third term for Obama!"

"In Benghazi, Hillary never showed up for the 3 AM call."

"The three most important problems are security, security, and security!"

"Many countries are not carrying their weight!"

Take Back Your News

"You always have to be prepared to walk away when you deal."

"I'll be slow on the trigger, but no one will mess with us."

"No one respects women more than Donald Trump!" although "these liars in the media behind you" won't say that.

Repeatedly he hit the national media. "I have the smartest people and the most loyal. Even the liars back there will say that."

And about Washington politicians, including the GOP establishment trying to derail his campaign, "Every single one of these people are controlling!"

Trump accused the GOP elite and pundits of saying he could not win the election, "but they said I couldn't win primaries either."

Donald Trump and Ted Cruz are different people with different skill sets but they share disdain directed at the Washington establishment where neither the ruling party nor the opposition can be trusted.

Vote in the Primary on Tuesday. It matters.

Appendices

Appendix 2 — State of the Union address

Following more than a year of critiques and coaching, wire service copy still needs daily editing to remove IEDs — Improvised Editing Devices — so readers get the news they deserve. The Wire Service version of the 2018 State of the Union Address, shows how copy still merits our concern. What follows first is the blue-penciled wire service version. Our complete rewrite follows that:

Headline: Trump calls for optimism in spite of warnings of danger

WASHINGTON — ~~Addressing a deeply divided nation,~~ President Donald Trump summoned the country to a "new American moment" of unity in his first State of the Union, challenging Congress to make good on long-standing promises to fix ~~a fractured~~the immigration system and warning ~~darkly~~ of evil forces seeking to undermine America's way of life.

Trump's address Tuesday night blended ~~self-congratulation and~~ calls for optimism amid a growing economy with ~~ominous~~ warnings about deadly gangs, the scourge of drugs and violent immigrants living in the United States illegally. ~~He cast the debate over immigration — an issue that has long animated his most ardent supporters — as a battle between heroes and villains, leaning heavily on the personal stories of White House guests in the crowd.~~ He praised a law enforcement agent who arrested more than 100 gang members, and he recognized the families of two alleged gang victims.

He also spoke ~~forebodingly~~ of ~~catastrophic~~ dangers from abroad, warning that North Korea would "very soon" threaten the United States with nuclear-tipped missiles.

"The United States is a compassionate nation. We are proud that we do more than any other country to help the needy, the struggling and the underprivileged all over the world," Trump said. "But as president of the United States, my highest loyalty, my greatest compassion, and my constant concern is for America's children, America's struggling workers and America's forgotten communities."

Trump addressed the nation with ~~tensions running high on Capitol Hill. An impasse over immigration prompted a three-day government shutdown earlier this year, and~~ lawmakers ~~appear~~ no closer to resolving the status of ~~the "Dreamers"~~ — young people living in the U.S. illegally ahead of a new Feb. 8 deadline for funding operations. The parties have also clashed this week over the plans of Republicans on the House intelligence committee to release a classified memo on the Russia investigation involving Trump's presidential campaign — a decision the White House backs but the Justice Department is fighting.

~~The controversies that have dogged Trump — and the ones he has created — have overshadowed strong economic gains during his first year in office. His~~

141

Take Back Your News

~~approval ratings have hovered in the 30s for much of his presidency, and just 3 in 10 Americans said the United States was heading in the right direction, according to a poll by The Associated Press-NORC Center for Public Affairs Research. In the same survey, 67 percent of Americans said the country was more divided because of Trump.~~

~~At times, Trump's address appeared to be aimed more at validating his first year in office than setting the course for his second.~~ He ~~devoted significant time to touting~~praised the tax overhaul he signed at the end of last year, promising the plan will "provide tremendous relief for the middle class and small businesses." He also highlighted the decision made early in his first year to withdraw the U.S. from a sweeping Asia-Pacific trade pact, declaring: "The era of economic surrender is totally over."

He spoke about potential agenda items for 2018 in broad terms, including a call for $1.5 trillion in new infrastructure spending and partnerships with states and the private sector. He touched only briefly on issues like health care ~~that have been at the center of the Republican Party's policy agenda for years.~~

~~Tackling the sensitive immigration debate that has roiled Washington,~~ Trump ~~redoubled~~ reiterated his recent pledge to offer a path to citizenship for 1.8 million young immigrants — but only as part of a package that would also require increased funding for border security, including a wall along the U.S.-Mexico border, ending the nation's visa lottery method and revamping the current legal immigration system. ~~Some Republicans are wary of the hardline elements of Trump's plan and it's unclear whether his blueprint could pass Congress.~~

"Americans are dreamers too," Trump said~~, in an apparent effort to reclaim the term used to describe the young immigrants in the U.S. illegally.~~

~~A former New York Democrat, the president also played to the culture wars that have long illuminated American politics, alluding to his public spat with professional athletes who led protests against racial injustice by kneeling during the national anthem, declaring that paying tribute to the flag is a "civic duty."~~

Republicans led multiple rounds of enthusiastic applause during the speech~~, but for the opposition party it was a more somber affair~~. Democrats provided a short spurt of polite applause for Trump as he entered the chamber, but offered muted reactions throughout the speech. ~~A cluster of about two dozen Democrats, including members of the Congressional Black Caucus, remained planted firmly in their seats, staring sternly at the president and withholding applause.~~

~~After devastating defeats in 2016, Democrats are hopeful that Trump's sagging popularity can help the party rebound in November's midterm elections.~~ In a post-speech rebuttal, Massachusetts Rep. Joe Kennedy~~, the grandson of Robert F. Kennedy,~~ was seeking to undercut Trump's optimistic tone and remind voters of the personal insults and attacks often leveled by the president.

~~"Bullies may land a punch," Kennedy said. "They might leave a mark. But they have never, not once, in the history of our United States, managed to match the strength and spirit of a people united in defense of their future."~~

The arc of Trump's 80-minute speech featured the personal stories of men and women who joined first lady Melania Trump in the audience. The guests included a New Mexico policeman and his wife who adopted a baby from parents who suffered from opioid addiction, and Ji Seong-ho, a defector from North Korea and outspoken critic of the Kim Jong-un government.

On international affairs, Trump warned of the dangers from "rogue regimes," like Iran and North Korea, terrorist groups, like the Islamic State, and "rivals" like China and Russia "that challenge our interests, our economy and our

Appendices

values." Calling on Congress to lift budgetary caps and boost spending on the military, Trump said that "unmatched power is the surest means of our defense."

Trump's biggest foreign policy announcement of the night concerned the Guantanamo Bay detention center, which former President Barack Obama tried but failed to close. Reversing Obama's policy, Trump said he'd signed an executive order Tuesday directing the Pentagon to keep the prison open while re-examining the military's policy on detention.

Trump said he was also asking Congress to ensure the U.S. had needed powers to detain Islamic State group members and other "terrorists wherever we chase them down.," ~~though it was unclear whether he was referring to a new war powers authorization or some other mechanism.~~ Trump also said he wanted Congress to pass a law ensuring U.S. foreign aid goes only "to America's friends" — a reference to his frustration at U.S. aid recipients that voted at the U.N. to rebuke his decision to recognize Jerusalem as Israel's capital.

~~Mrs. Trump arrived at the Capitol ahead of her husband to attend a reception with guests of the White House, but she rode back to the White House with him. It was the first time she was seen publicly with the president following a report that his lawyer arranged a payment to a porn star, Stormy Daniels, to prevent her from talking about an alleged affair. Daniels denied the affair in a new statement released hours before the speech.~~

The article that follows is our reporting of the State of the Union address:

Headline: Trump: Union is strong because people are strong

WASHINGTON — In his first State of the Union address, President Donald Trump defined his mission, measured the milestones for his first year in office, and set goals for Congress. Trump said his mission was to make America great again for all Americans.

He said the state of the union is strong because Americans are strong. He complimented the steel spines of Americans like the informal Cajun Navy that rescued many in recent hurricanes and first responders who saved lives in the Las Vegas mass shooting.

Trump listed 2.4 million more jobs, including many in manufacturing, rising wages, a 45-year low for unemployment claims, African-American and Hispanic jobless claims at the lowest levels ever recorded, and an $8 trillion increase in the stock market that has raised the value of 401(k), retirement accounts, and college savings plans.

He said that April will be the last time taxpayers file returns under the old system, the tax of government-ordered health care has been eliminated, and corporate and small business taxes have been reduced.

He challenged Congress to empower agencies to reward good workers and remove bad ones.

To make Washington accountable, Trump said his administration had removed wasteful regulations. There have been, he said, more FDA drug approvals than ever before, but he wants to reduce the cost of prescription drugs and allow access to experimental drugs for patients with terminal diseases.

He proposed immigration policies that support what he said are the best interests of Americans, closing open borders that have allowed in gangs.

To support his case, guests in the gallery included two families whose daughters had been murdered by illegal unaccompanied alien minors.

He proposed to work with both parties to protect all children of every color and creed, stating that the United States is a compassionate nation, but his highest loyalty is for America children, struggling workers, and communities, adding, "Americans are dreamers, too."

He offered a path to citizenship for 1.8 million immigrants — three times more people than the previous administration, over a 12-year period. The other pillars to his proposal were a fully secured border, the end of catch and release, an end the visa lottery without regard for skill, merit, or safety, and an end to chain migration to focus on immediate family, ending unlimited entry.

Abroad, Trump said that ISIS had lost almost 100 percent of its territory. He wanted Guantanamo Bay kept open for terrorists as unlawful enemy combatants. He set new rules of engagement, recognized Jerusalem, and wants $20 billion on foreign aid conditioned on support of American policies.

Trump said he wants to restore clarity about foreign policy. America stands with people of Iran, Cuba, Venezuela and North Korea. About Korea, he said past experience shows that complacency and concession don't work.

Trump ended by reminding Congress that 250 years ago the country's founders had the revolutionary idea that they could rule themselves and that the Capitol is a monument to American people.

Trump said people living "all around us" are responsible for "defending hope, pride, and the American way." He added, "And this capitol, city, nation, belongs entirely to them. Our task is to respect them, to listen to them, to serve them, to protect them, and to always be worthy of them."

He closed saying, "The people dreamed this country. The people built this country. And it is the people who are making America great again."

In a post-speech rebuttal, Democratic Massachusetts Rep. Joe Kennedy sought to undercut Trump's tone and remind voters of the way Trump has responded to critics.

Appendix 3 — Questions that nurture thinking

The current fad would have authorities consciously create consensus. Presuming to know the consensus to create is the kind of hubris faced down repeatedly over 25 centuries. Confucius, Socrates, Ibn Khaldun, Matthew Arnold, among others challenged those who promoted authority and politically correct social conformity at the expense of individual engagement.

Confucius promoted individual thinking skills to engage family, friends, community, and authority because decisions left to others cause people to lose contact with what matters.

Sidestep the tussle over what to teach. Nudge students to develop the ability to think analytically so they can engage themselves to answer why what seemed valuable to our predecessors might still matter. Each generation has to revalidate principles so teachers directed by authorities cannot enslave them.

Book 2 examined how a government-fostered lens called "critical thinking" elbowed aside sound material in history, economics, and political theory to promote docile compliancy.

Golden threads extracted from experience begin with a sense of time and one's place in it. *A Street Through Time*[53] engages even young students in the arc of experience to mine it for useful patterns and exercise their tools for thought.

Follow that with good questions. There are so many, but samples will get the conversation rolling:

History
- What is the value of history?
    > History is not a straightforward uncomplicated narrative but an exercise in making and remaking choices.[54]

---

[53] Millard, Anne and Steve Noon. *A Street Through Time*. 2012. DK Publishing. New York.
[54] Allen C. Guelzo, Civil War professor, Gettysburg College.

- How do you distinguish between events and the history written about those events?
    > History writing is a humanistic prose narrative of events based on systematic inquiry into words, deeds, ideas, conflicts, and sufferings that occurred in the past and that left verifiable evidentiary trails in the present.[55]
- If the late 1800s were the period of robber barons taking advantage of needy people, and if it was also a time when immigrants with nothing could build a life and advance their children, what represents the history of the period and what lesson should be learned? Would today's laws allow the kind of advancement possible in the 1890s?

Economics

- Is capitalism as a political theory too important to leave to Economics?
- What is required for capitalism to succeed?
- How may capitalism vary—entrepreneurial, dynamic, democratic or nondemocratic, competitive or state driven?
- Should commercial exchange be voluntary or mandatory?
    > Commerce is voluntary but government is mandatory.
- Do price signals matter?
    > Price signals may be masked by tax policy, price fixing, or by government control. When might such things be good policy?
- Along the continuum between globalism and nationalism what makes the most sense and how should one decide?
- Does capitalism break down barriers or encourage them?
- How do capitalism and enforced equality compare?
- Should a state seek equality of result or equality of opportunity?
- Adam Smith's 1776 *Wealth of Nations* was an attack on the government controls of his time—mercantilism, tariffs, and government monopoly—but aren't those the results today's reformers seek?
- If people, as individuals do what works best for themselves, what does government do?
- Since people and businesses adapt to whatever the tax code is or becomes, what should the tax code do? What direction for a tax code would be productive? How does one crate a tax code that won't be hijacked by special interests?

Political theory

- What is the purpose of government?

---

[55] Ibid.

Appendices

> To do for individuals what they cannot reasonably do for themselves. Common defense. Enforce contracts ... — Adam Smith

- Who should set the goals for society, government of individuals? How should such goals be set.
- Should society tend toward being free or managed?
- If government is supposed to be of the people, by the people, and for the people, who are the people?
- What protections should people have from government run by other people?
- Does an elected representative represent district voters or the entire country?
- Does federalism that encourages competition benefit people more than top-down uniform compliance?
- Absent federalism, what checks exist to protect against governmental abuse?
- What are the requirements for a geographic area to expect independence? Economic self-sufficiency? What else?
- Can individuals participate in community and retain individuality?
- Is capitalism more a destroyer of traditional communities or a creator of news communities?
- Should societies base themselves primarily on trade?
- Is regimentation or liberty better for the good of society, and what is the good of society?
- How much national income should be spent by the state? What should national income be spent on?

  > According to Milton Friedman, in 1928, less than 10% was spent on all government and 2/3 of that was state and local. In 1977, 40% was spent on all government and 2/3 of that was federal.

- How does market-orientation affect household distribution of time/effort?
- Should competition be open or secret, under cover of government?

Science

- What is science?

  > An ongoing process that compares experience with hypotheses, pruning away what is demonstrably wrong.

- What is there to learn about past attempts to claim science was settled like Galileo's theories?

www.ingramcontent.com/pod-product-compliance
Lightning Source LLC
Chambersburg PA
CBHW030936090426
42737CB00007B/451